Positive Affirmations For Black Woman

959 Daily Powerful & Inspirational
Affirmations for BIPOC Women to Attract
Happiness, Health and Success.
Boost Your Confidence & Self-Love to Live in
Abundance

Malika Nkoulou

Table of Contents

Introduction

This book will be about positive affirmations for black women. It will explore the factors that contribute to black women not feeling confident and how proper self-care is important for them to feel worthy of success. It will cover various topics such as self-care and how it can positively affect a person and the importance of understanding that not all discrimination experienced by black people is negative. It will also touch on using affirmations to uplift oneself and others. Lastly, it looks at how this can make a difference for black women in their relationships with others. These affirmations will give black women hope that they can accomplish their goals and achieve anything they set their mind to, even if life has dealt them the short end of the stick.

Black women are often made to feel inferior to everyone because of many stereotypes about them. They are not always treated respectfully, and it is common for them to think that they have less than others, even though there is very little wrong with them. For black women to feel worthy of success, they need to look at themselves and what can be done better. This book will give them the tools they need with the hopes that it will help them succeed.

There are many ways in which one may want to use affirmations. Each person has their way of using these strategies. Some people like to repeat them aloud, while others prefer to say them in their minds. Some people find writing them down on a piece of paper and placing the paper somewhere where they will see it often is the best option. This way, they are written down before them, so they cannot forget them.

Those who have used affirmations feel that positive thinking can be used to overcome any obstacle, as long as one truly believes it. Affirmations are a great way to help someone focus on all of the good things about themself and how precisely they can achieve their goals and dreams. They can be used by those seeking to learn how to make better choices or those who want to be more positive or happier. They can also be used to help someone conquer negative thoughts about themselves. They may also be used by people trying to become more successful in their chosen careers.

If one is unhappy, it can be difficult for that person alone, but affirmations also help people who have problems. It gives them hope and a positive outlook on life, and they feel that they have the ability to overcome any obstacle that they may face. Those who feel that they are in a negative place due to the influence of others or because of their feelings are trying to find ways to bring about change or at least feel better about themselves. They try to change their outlook and use affirmations to make any changes that they wish to make.

People who use positive thinking will find many benefits when using this form of self-care. It gives them a sense of control over every situation they may find themselves in. It also helps them to feel better about themselves and their lives. They believe that they can do anything and that nothing is impossible. They also think that they are worthy of success and know that they deserve to reach the heights of any mountain they may choose to climb. Those who use affirmations want to be surrounded by positive people and want them to believe the same way so that it becomes a true possibility in their lives. They want those around them to know how much it will mean if they say encouraging things or help them in any way possible. It helps those using these strategies because it gives them a sense of peace and calmness.

There are various myths surrounding the black community and African Americans in general. One such myth is that black people have never contributed to society or made any contributions to society. I plan to address this misconception and others like it by showing that black people have made numerous contributions throughout history and in every area of society. In addition, I plan on showing how these contributions have affected the lives of others. This can help break the negative stigma surrounding black people and help them better understand their culture and the people who come from it.

By understanding the positive contributions that have been made, black women will be more likely to find the motivation they need to succeed in life and their relationships. They will be able to eliminate some of the negativity surrounding them and realize how capable of achieving greatness they are. A large part of this will be done by removing these negative stereotypes surrounding black people and replacing them with positive affirmations that they can take with them throughout their daily lives. I hope that the positive affirmations I present in this book will help you achieve your goals and do great things. I hope to inspire you and share my advice with you. If there is anything I can improve on or add, let me know in the comments.

The process of making this book was not easy. There are so many different topics that could have been covered and many different avenues for which I could have gone about it. I want to thank all my teachers who helped me learn about various topics, such as history and psychology, and various people who helped me develop this book idea. This is just scratching the surface of all the things that went into making this book possible. I also want to thank all my classmates who helped test out the affirmations and helped me improve them.

I hope this book will help you develop positive habits and change your thinking to achieve your goals. If you are still reading and interested in self-development, I hope this book serves as an inspiration and motivator to help you achieve your life goals. As we continue down the path of self-improvement, we will make positive changes for ourselves and others.

Chapter 1: What Are Positive Affirmations and How They Work

Positive affirmations are phrases that you repeat to yourself when you need encouragement or are in a low mood. Positive affirmations use words and images that promote self-acceptance and show what we want to create in our lives. As children, most of us heard phrases like "you can't do it" or "don't be so stupid" from adults. These messages are often repeated in our heads on a loop during difficult times, causing feelings of inadequacy and worthlessness. Positive affirmations are the antidote for these negative voices in your head. You can repeat them repeatedly, and you will begin to believe them. The return is that when you think of yourself in negative ways, you start to change the words and images in your mind. You create new affirmations about yourself, about the things you want to make for your life.

Positive affirmations are a great way to strengthen your confidence and self-esteem. If you have been raised with negative messages from others, you must take the time to turn them around in your mind. Regardless of our race or gender, we all receive messages about our value from others. We receive messages about being worthless and bad all of our life, yet we can rise above this if we want to change.

Positive affirmations remind us of who we are and what we want to create in our lives. If you had ideas, visions, hopes and dreams as a young person, take the time to reclaim them. Learn how to be the person you want to be. Affirm yourself when you need support or encouragement. Talking to ourselves is the only way for us to change the voice in our heads that says we are unworthy or bad. The main question is, "am I talking to myself in a confidence-promoting way?"

Let me give an example: If you want to feel good about yourself, tell yourself at least three times a day that you are important and beautiful no matter what anyone else says. You are not worthless or bad. You are important and valuable, especially for you! Go for it! Be consistent by aiming your affirmations at your heart as much as possible, then repeat them aloud. When you hear negative thoughts and voices in your mind, remind yourself that they are all false. Repeat positive affirmations to yourself until they become a part of who you are and what you want in life. The most important step is to accept yourself as a valued human being.

By repeating positive affirmations daily, you begin to change your beliefs about yourself and create new ones about your life and experiences. You also change what you are thinking about yourself and your life. You begin to see your worthiness and value differently. Tell yourself that you are an amazing person who has value and worth each day. You deserve love, friendship, peace of mind and happiness in your life! Affirm it repeatedly until it becomes a part of who you are!

The great thing is that positive affirmations feel good when we use them. You will swear by them as you see your life move forward. Your mind is very powerful so use it to your advantage. Feel good about yourself and be happy; talk to yourself confidently and encouragingly. Affirm that you are important, valuable and deserving of a great life.

If you want to change in your life, if you want to feel better about yourself, be consistent with your affirmations or positive statements about what YOU CAN DO or BE! Say them consistently for at least twenty minutes a day for the next two weeks.

Whenever I feel down or negative, I use positive affirmations to shake myself out. It has made a huge difference in my life. It has strengthened my confidence in myself and my abilities. Here are some positive affirmations that have been helpful for me: "I deserve happiness." "I'm okay as I am." "Life is good!" "The world is a wonderful place. I enjoy living." "The universe is abundant. The more I have, the more I can give." "I know what's best for me." "I enjoy life and living fully in the present moment!" If you feel negative or depressed and are looking for an antidote to these feelings, I highly recommend using positive affirmations. They do work!

Positive affirmations work in our minds and can bring about positive change in your life. If you use them consistently, they will help you create the life you want. Your thoughts, beliefs and attitudes are all a part of this equation. When you use positive affirmations every day, they will become a way of life for you and a way to achieve the goals you want to reach.

Positive affirmations focus on what we want rather than what we don't want. In addition, positive affirmations bring our attention back to something good in our lives that we might have forgotten or overlooked. Affirmations are one way to work on our inner selves to take a positive approach. When we feel negative about something, we use affirmations to change our thinking and attitudes. They help us focus on the positive steps we can take rather than the negative ones.

If you want to succeed at anything, you have to believe that it is possible and believe in yourself. Affirmations are a great way to do this. Positive affirmations help us begin believing in ourselves and what we want. Positive affirmations are statements we can use to help us to promote our energy and new ideas. They also give us a chance to change our life by using different words and images in our minds. Your mind is very powerful, so you need to take the time to learn how to use it positively.

The best way for me is with positive affirmations. I repeat them repeatedly, whether aloud or just in my mind. It doesn't have the same effect if you tell yourself the same thing only once or twice a day. If you do that, you will lose power because your brain will stop hearing them after a while! You must be persistent and consistent when using affirmations.

I have been using affirmations for several years. It's amazing how positive I have been able to change through them. Affirmations allow us to truly believe in ourselves, learn and grow as a person and improve our happiness levels (especially when we use them repeatedly). Affirmations are a great tool that can help you achieve your dreams. They work! If you want advice, I suggest using positive affirmations to become more confident in yourself and what you are doing with your life. Also, remember that it's okay to say yes even when you're scared or unsure!

Many people can use affirmations. You'll begin seeing results within the first day or two – if not sooner. It's also very wise to begin using affirmations daily. That way, you will start to believe in your abilities, and you won't ever have doubts about yourself or what you are doing. You will go forward with your goals, even when you face problems or challenges – because of the power of positive affirmations and the belief they give us.

I prefer reading positive affirmations aloud; it is more effective than reading them to yourself. This is a great way to get an immediate positive "feel" for what a positive affirmation will feel like. It is more like a positive experience than reading words on a page. I also like to create short affirmations, keep it simple and always use the present tense. Use your imagination and develop fun, empowering affirmations to repeat aloud. If you prefer not to say them aloud, that's okay too – but be sure to read them out loud somehow so you can experience the sounds of the words.

Affirmations are very powerful tools that help us in many ways. They allow us to get rid of unwanted feelings and beliefs. They help us move up our happiness levels by making us more positive in our attitude towards life and more confident about our lives and future. When we use affirmations, we can control our emotions and thoughts. We can replace negative thoughts with positive ones and make more rational decisions to succeed in life.

Suppose you love someone developing an exercise program. In that case, you could suggest that they use the following positive affirmation: "I am the type of person who maintains an active lifestyle by doing regular physical activity regularly." It's also good to share some tips on how they can keep their fitness goals in mind during their day. Write down your objectives related to your goals and read them during your commute or before breakfast! Remember, people develop healthy habits because they enjoy doing what they choose. So, if you can help your loved one enjoy a fitness routine, it will become much more likely that they will keep doing it.

I also recommend affirmations to help us check our thoughts and correct them if necessary. You can use the following sentence in that situation: "I can think of a positive thought because I am focused on the positive aspects of my life." You may not always be able to find a better thought, but you can make sure your original thought is positive. Positive emotions are an essential part of living a happy life, so try to make them a priority and never forget about them.

Affirmations can help you get rid of negative thinking, which helps us be more productive at work. We should use affirmations as motivation because we want to succeed in all areas of our lives. If we're going to be more confident about our decisions, we can say the following affirmation: "I am someone who makes decisions based on rational thoughts and not emotions." If you often worry about bad things occurring in your life, try using the following affirmation instead: "I can relax because my life is going well." Whenever you worry about something, tell yourself one of these positive affirmations. It will help bring you peace of mind and allow you to focus on more important things in your life.

Chapter 2: Benefits of Positive Affirmations

Positive affirmations help improve self-esteem, while they also help to alleviate symptoms of depression and anxiety. If you've been going through a tough time, you might want to try this quick and easy five-minute routine! Make sure not to repeat the mantra too long. It's better to repeat it only a few times.

By repeating positive affirmations, you'll realize real and lasting results in a short time. Don't expect overnight changes, though. This exercise is more like a high-intensity round of slow weight lifting. Make sure you're in the right frame of mind before you start. I'd advise you to use the mantra "I'm beautiful." It will help with positive self-talk and self-esteem-boosting affirmations that will help uplift your mood and eliminate negative thought patterns and behaviors.

Positive affirmations also improve your energy level and help alleviate symptoms of depression and anxiety. When you start to feel down, you'll be able to use these positive statements as a way of self-talk to cheer yourself up.

Positive affirmations are designed to help you break free from the negative thoughts and behaviors that control your life. You can consciously choose what you want or need in your life. By affirming that you have what it takes to make your dreams happen, you will be confident in what you're doing.

You can use positive affirmations to help you express your feelings. When you begin to feel unhappy or depressed, try creating these positive statements as a way of helping yourself in the way of expression and confidence. Expressing yourself through positive affirmations is a healthier way to deal with issues and feelings.

- By saying positive affirmations, you'll be able to get rid of the negative thoughts and self-doubts holding you back from success.

- Positive affirmations will enable you to feel self-confidence and love for yourself. When you feel good about yourself, others will too! Being confident in yourself will attract people to you, both personally and professionally. It's a great feeling!

- Positive thoughts will help build your self-esteem, while they can help to release tension in your body.

- Positive affirmations will help you to rid yourself of negative behaviors and thoughts. With this, you'll be able to live a happier life and draw people towards you positively.

- Positive affirmations help you to come across as being confident in what you are doing. This will make others more confident in working with you!

- By saying positive affirmations, you'll be able to give yourself a sounding board for your ideas and advice. You can also use these positive messages to express your feelings as well. If you're feeling unhappy, this exercise can help! It's also a great way to alleviate stress and negative symptoms that may be bothering you.

- Positive affirmations will help you break free from the negative thoughts and behaviors that control your life. You can consciously choose what you want or need in your life. By affirming that you have what it takes to make your dreams happen, you will be confident in what you're doing.

- Try saying positive affirmations out loud instead of just thinking about them. The words become more real when heard! This helps to expand on the positive meaning behind the thought or affirmation. You'll find that saying affirmations aloud can help you feel better about yourself and your life.

- Positive affirmations also improve your energy level and help alleviate symptoms of depression and anxiety. When you start to feel down, you'll be able to use these positive statements as a way of self-talk to cheer yourself up.

- By repeating positive affirmations, you'll be able to work on a stricter area of your life every day! You can also say these phrases out loud instead of silently repeating them in your head.

- Repeat positive affirmations often. It's best to repeat them forty times or once every morning and night while saying the words at least twice. Try doing this with positive statements such as "I'm happy. I love myself. I'm healthy. I'm successful. I have good friends."

- Make sure you're in the right frame of mind before you start. I'd advise you to use the mantra "I'm beautiful". It will help with positive self-talk and self-esteem-boosting affirmations that will help uplift your mood and eliminate negative thought patterns and behaviors. If, for some reason, this mantra doesn't work for you or feels weird, change it! Find a positive affirmation that fits you best. Repeat this several times every day.

- Repeat positive affirmations after reading them a few times. You can use the mantra "I'm beautiful" for this exercise. Once you've read it a few times, do not think about the meaning behind the words or try to analyze what it means for yourself. Just say the words repeatedly, as many times as you can! This is a very good way to get rid of anxiety and stress and to help lift your spirits!

- Make sure you're in a positive frame of mind when you say these statements. It's hard for negative thoughts to creep in if your intentions are positive. Also, try to think of positive things currently happening in your life. You can do this using the mantra: "I'm happy. I love myself." It can help you remember important events and milestones that have taken place in your life.

- Use positive affirmations when you're feeling down. This will take away the negative feelings and lift your spirits! By repeating positive affirmations, you'll be able to support yourself and help yourself to come out of the negatives.

- If you're short of time or having trouble remembering your positive affirmations, write them down on a piece of paper and keep it in a convenient place so that they can be used at any time. This can help with keeping track of what it is that you want in your life! You can write down a few positive affirmations on one sheet or use several sheets. Either way, you should have the time to get through them all!

- It's best if you say these positive affirmations out loud. This will help you to focus on the positive meaning behind the thoughts and words and help you come across as being positive. When saying affirmations out loud, it's also much easier for them to become real in your mind.

- It can be beneficial to repeat these positive affirmations once a week. You can do this by saying them out loud while thinking of your life goals simultaneously. This is a great way of ensuring that you do what it takes to make your dreams come true.

- Focus on the positive. Focus on positive feelings and emotions instead of negative ones. You can use positive affirmations to talk to yourself and express your feelings! Say these words out loud to better connect with them. You can also write them down to return to them repeatedly.

- When repeating positive affirmations, please focus on the words without worrying about what they mean or what you want, or need in your life. If you're worried about their meaning, try saying the mantra "I'm happy" or "I love myself". This way, you're not worrying about it so much.

- Don't worry if your first few attempts at repeating positive affirmations do not work out. It's best if you keep trying until you get it right!

- The only thing that should matter when repeating these positive affirmations is real and come from the heart. So, repeat them with a positive attitude and with enthusiasm. Don't think about what you're saying in your mind; instead, think about what you want or need in your life without considering what the words mean! It's best to say these words out loud as well. You can do this by writing them down or repeating them to yourself.

- Stay positive while thinking of your life goals. These are the things you want to achieve, and each one should have specific meaning for you, your health, education and happiness.

- If you're having trouble with positive affirmations, think of your life goals. This will help you think positive thoughts and help you see why it is that you need to be repeating these affirmations.

- It's best if your positive affirmation contains a number that signifies a goal for yourself. You can use a number such as 1 or 2 or 4, etc., and add this number to a phrase that has meaning for you or includes your goals. For example, if the first thing on your life goals list is "to own my own house", try repeatedly saying, "I will own my own house in one year.

- Positive affirmations can help you create the life you want, and if you are in a relationship, that isn't all it could be, then positive affirmations can help with that. Creating an abundant life takes more than just saying affirmations over and over. It takes a great deal of thought and dedication to become a person who believes in the power of positive thinking and having the courage to try new things, but perhaps most importantly, it requires action on your part. Here are some examples of what you can tell yourself to get started with using positive affirmations for specific results.

Positive affirmations can be powerful tools for personal transformation. If you want to change your life and the lives of others positively, try some of the examples listed above, or create your affirmations based on your specific needs. Accuracy is important when using affirmations, so if you aren't sure how something is supposed to sound, it's best to either write down the words exactly as they sound or have someone read them to you until they have memorized them. This will help to ensure that you are communicating what you mean in a positive way. When it comes to realizing your dreams and creating an abundant life, positive thinking can be one of your greatest assets. Positive affirmations or positive thinking can help one achieve goals. Also, it can help you keep a positive attitude when going through a hard period. For example, if you want to lose weight, you need to think positively about yourself, and others will see your efforts positively and support you in your goals

Chapter 3: Positive Affirmations for Self-Love

Positive affirmations for self-love can be very powerful. They are words that we repeat to ourselves when feeling most insecure, sad, or scared. The idea behind positive affirmations is that you will eventually believe it to be true by repeating the affirmation repeatedly in your mind. It may take a lot of practice to get used to saying these affirmations and not only believing them but feeling them. Sometimes it just takes an extra push of confidence or a reminder every day for us to feel good about ourselves and our lives.

Positive affirmations for us are a great way to start that push. By using positive affirmations, we can remind ourselves of all the good things in our lives and all the good things we offer. Positive affirmations can help us bring our self-love to the forefront and priorities it. What positive affirmations do is that they remind us of the good things, good things that are all around us, good things that we are capable of.

It is also very much about being positive; if; if you focus on all the negative in your life, you might as well give up. Positive affirmation is not about ignoring or forgetting anything. It is about adding in the positive so that you balance it out.

If you are feeling down, lost, or need a reminder of your good qualities, try repeating the positive affirmations out loud or in your mind. Over time you will retrain your mind and start to believe that it is true. You can also use positive affirmations whenever you feel that you need a boost of confidence and some motivation to help yourself through a hard time or a challenge at work or with friends and family.

Self-love is not selfish. You are an important part of this world, and there is room for you to love yourself and take care of yourself, just like there is room for you to help others. There is nothing wrong with being there for yourself. The journey to better self-love is important, and it doesn't have to belong. Positive affirmations can help you get started on being a happier person. To truly believe that you are worthy of love, affirm it every day until you believe it.

Positive Affirmations for Self-Love:

1. I am worthy of love.
2. I am a good person.
3. I am kind.
4. I am perfect.
5. I am beautiful.
6. I am loved.
7. I am valuable.
8. Good things happen to me.
9. I am strong.
10. The universe loves me.
11. I am peaceful.
12. I am generous.
13. I am a good mother/father.
14. I and others are safe.
15. I have a purpose in life.
16. None of my dreams is impossible to achieve.
17. I deserve happiness
18. I am capable of greatness.
19. I am unique.
20. I love and forgive myself.
21. My heart is open to receiving the good things in life. I am thankful for the beauty in my life, and I give thanks for it every day.
22. None of my dreams is impossible to achieve
23. My heart is open to receiving the good things in life, and I give thanks for them every day.
24. The universe loves me; I have a meaningful future before me
25. My soul is filled with peace and joy, always.
26. All my interactions with others are filled with love.
27. I deserve the best.
28. I can attract positivity into my life.
29. I enjoy each day as it comes.
30. I love myself.
31. I appreciate other people, and I show it.
32. My life has meaning; whether others see it, I know that what I'm doing is worth my time.

33. All my interactions with others are filled with love and kindness, always.
34. I deserve to be happy.
35. I love myself, and I show it to others.
36. I treat others with dignity and respect because that is how I would like to be treated.
37. I have a bright future ahead of me!
38. All my interactions with others are filled with love and kindness; all the time.
39. What is beautiful brings joy.
40. What is beautiful in me brings joy to those around me.
41. I am happy when I see beauty in others; a smile on their face or the way they hold themselves, what they are wearing, and how they speak, walk and move to tell something about who they are.
42. I want the best for myself and the best for others.
43. We are all perfectly complete in our way; no one is meant to be like anyone else.
44. I deserve to feel good about myself.
45. I am happy and content.
46. People like me, and they appreciate who I am.
47. I am a loyal partner.
48. I know what I want, and I know that I deserve it.
49. I am comfortable with myself and my decisions.
50. All is well in my world.
51. My thoughts are aligned with universal good. Therefore, everything in my life is working out for the best.
52. I trust myself and trust the universe.
53. I have faith that the right people will show up at exactly the right time
54. When we love ourselves, we can be better parents, partners, friends and business colleagues; this will ultimately help us have a better life experience overall.
55. When we love ourselves, the world becomes a more beautiful place.
56. When we love ourselves, we are free to love others.
57. When we love ourselves, we allow others to be far more accepting of us than when they look at us as a means to an end.

58. The greatest gift that I can give myself and others is love, so I choose this as my goal in life.
59. My passion for life is revealed in living my life in harmony with the Divine within me and without me wherever I am, whatever I am doing. Choosing joy is the cornerstone to living my passion for life.
60. People treat me well, and I treat them kindly in return.
61. People accept me and love me for who I am.
62. Other people are my greatest teachers, and I listen to them.
63. I make clear and specific goals for myself and then achieve them.
64. I am in the right place at the right time.
65. I trust my inner guidance system with all my heart and soul.
66. My life overflows with meaning, purpose, peace, joy, fun and abundance.
67. All is well in my world!
68. To be successful, I start by believing in myself; when we believe that we can do something, it becomes easier to succeed than if we think that we cannot do it; self-confidence is essential to being successful.
69. When we like ourselves, we treat ourselves in good ways, and other people will like us and be more likely to treat us well.
70. When we like ourselves, it is easier to change the things in our lives that are not working to achieve what is important to us.
71. We have a lot of power over the quality of our own lives; if we think positive thoughts and have a positive attitude, this will help us succeed at whatever we are trying to do. We create a virtuous cycle of achievement by having a positive self-image and being optimistic about what can be accomplished.
72. People support me, encourage me, care for me, and show true compassion for my troubles.
73. I am worthy.
74. I feel thankful that I am healthy and can enjoy every day.
75. I appreciate the beautiful nature around me.
76. I wake up every day appreciating the beauty I see in my surroundings.
77. I appreciate the light that I see the first thing in the morning. It gives me energy and empowers me to be the person I know I can be.

78. I love spending time outside every day and seeing the magic of nature that is all around me.
79. I am happy, and I love life.

~~~~

Some of these affirmations are about what you want, and others are about what you deserve. Still, regardless of the type of affirmation, positive affirmations are powerful medicine for your self-love, as it gives us all a boost of confidence when we need it most. When you feel a little low and don't feel like the best version of yourself, repeat these affirmations. They are there for you to use to draw from every day. Use them throughout your day as often as possible to become engrained in your mind and soul.

Positive self-affirmations will tell us that we are worth it; we deserve it. Self-love is important because self-love can give us positive energy and motivation to do better things and make changes that will eventually create healthier habits and relationships. It can help us create confidence; it can make us feel stronger, better and more capable of making the right decisions. These affirmations are there to remind you of the good things in life and that you are someone worthwhile.

I am a good person

Positive self-affirmations are also about being a good person. We live in a world where people judge others based on their looks or how much money they have, but positive affirmations are about truth. They tell us that we can be successful if we do the right thing and always treat others the way we want them to. Treating others the same way we want to be treated is what positive affirmations are all about.

I am kind

Positive self-affirmations are about being kind, respectful and helpful. Being treated the way you want to be is something those positive affirmations are all about. By treating other people in the way you would like them to treat you, by being respectful and giving your time and attention when someone needs it, by respecting other people's beliefs or opinions, these things teach us that we can be a good people even if we are not perfect. These affirmations teach us that being kind is more important than ever before.

Positive self-affirmations are about being happy and content. Having someone you can depend on, someone who loves you for who you are and cares about your well-being. Positive affirmations are about being kind to yourself by taking time to write in a journal, meditating, going for a walk or spending time with people you love. These things will make you happier, showing you what it means to be happy. Positive affirmations are all about being able only to think positive things and letting go of the negative feelings. Positive affirmations teach us that we can be happy even when everything is not the way we want it to be.

I am a good friend

Positive self-affirmations are about being a good friend. Friendships are often hard to maintain, and if we aren't feeling as good as we'd like to be, it cannot be easy to create a healthy friendship. Positive affirmations will remind you that you deserve love and respect in your relationships, that you can be a good friend and that our happiness is important in every relationship. Positive affirmations will remind us of the benefits of being a good friend because loving others is the best thing we can do for ourselves.

I am attractive

Positive self-affirmations are about believing that you are attractive, desirable and beautiful even though everyone around you might disagree with this idea. Becoming comfortable with yourself, and being happy with everything you have, is a big step toward believing that you are attractive. Working on your self-esteem through positive affirmations will help you make changes in your life. It can make you a stronger person. Positive affirmations teach us that we can be beautiful even if we don't have the perfect body or perfect face.

I am beautiful

Positive self-affirmations are about believing that we are beautiful and glowing with happiness. Positive affirmations tell us that we can still feel beautiful even when everything is wrong and only feel anything negative. Positive affirmations tell us that we can feel beautiful after a bad day or when we have lost everything. Positive affirmations tell us that self-love is the most important thing we have because by loving ourselves, we can be more confident, and we will shine even in the darkest situations.

Positive self-affirmations are about believing that you are capable of being great. Becoming comfortable with your faults and flaws is one of the most important things you can do for yourself; it can make you a better person. Positive affirmations are about having faith in yourself and your abilities; they teach us to believe that we can achieve anything we want. Positive affirmations are all about you believing in your worthiness. Positive affirmations teach us that we can always do great things.

I deserve better

Positive self-affirmations are about believing that you deserve better than what you have. Everyone deserves happiness; everyone deserves to have a place that they feel worthy of calling their own. If you are unhappy, start with positive affirmations and make them your work of duty. Positive affirmations will teach you that you deserve everything that makes you happy.

Chapter 4: Positive Affirmations for Mind & Body

If you struggle with confidence or self-worth, it might not be easy to believe that you deserve positivity. Take some time out of your day to fully focus on the positive affirmations in this post when you start repeating them to yourself, meditation by reminding yourself of these people who have helped you before. Look at the picture of them and feel their support.

Make sure to keep them in a place where you can see them often. You can have a mirror where you can see them, keep the affirmations on your phone, or post it up somewhere you know they won't get lost. Your mind is a powerful tool. You can use it to create positive affirmations. When your mind starts to wander, bring yourself back into the moment by repeating a positive affirmation over in your head. When you can focus on them, write them down and look at them daily. You might need to keep a journal or start writing in one. This will help you see how far you have come, and you can track this progress.

You might want to take some time out with yourself, do something that pleases you, focus on how good it feels, and treat yourself like a queen. You will be amazed at how much more confident, happy and loved you feel when you become aware. You have the power to change your life, and you need to start by believing it. You are loved and capable of great things. I believe in you!

Positive affirmations for mind & body:

1. I am well-accepted and well-respected.
2. I have a healthy and beautiful body.
3. My future will be prosperous.
4. I am confident, competent, and capable.
5. I radiate strength and beauty from the inside out.
6. I am loved and valued.
7. I believe in myself and my ability to make it happen.
8. I am a worthy, productive, contributing member of society.
9. I have the energetic vibrations of happiness and prosperity.

10. I have a healthy and confident self-image.
11. I have good health and a positive outlook on life.
12. I am connected to the Divine Source of Love & Light that exists within me & beyond me. I have the wisdom & know-how to do what I desire.
13. I have all the resources in my life to accomplish my goals and dreams.
14. I am energetically connected to the divine source of unconditional love & bliss
15. I am a competent, capable, and resourceful person.
16. I trust in my ability to achieve my goals.
17. I am surrendering to the universe and letting go of control.
18. I relax with no anxiety or self-judgment.
19. I am healthy, happy, and at peace.
20. I am confident and secure in knowing that my potential is infinite.
21. I find joy in life and myself.
22. The universe is working with me to achieve my goals, dreams & desires.
23. My intuition and guidance are extremely reliable.
24. I have a strong desire to make all my dreams come true.
25. I attract new opportunities into my life.
26. I trust in the universe's flow, trusting that it will take care of me.
27. I'm excited about my future, just as enthusiastic about my past.
28. My intuitive intelligence and self-healing abilities are vital.
29. I trust in the Divine Power of Life, Love & Light.
30. I am healthy and full of joy.
31. I am confident, capable and competent.
32. Inner peace pervades all that I do.
33. The Universe is working with me to achieve my goals, dreams and desires.
34. I trust in my intuition and have faith in the processes of life.
35. I am inspired and uplifted by life's infinite possibilities.
36. I am confident that everything will come to fruition most beautifully.
37. I feel a sense of well-being. A wonderful feeling of peace, happiness, and oneness with the universe.
38. I believe that things can always get better.

39. I am happy, healthy, and motivated.
40. I accept all responsibility for my actions and failures.
41. I can handle the responsibilities needed to make all my dreams come true.
42. I trust in myself to do what is needed to be successful.
43. My finances are stable or increasing.
44. Each day, I am growing and becoming a complete person in each way.
45. I am thankful for all the pleasure, love, and joy I have in my life.
46. I have the wisdom to know what to do.
47. I accept myself unconditionally.
48. My intuition and guidance are extremely reliable.
49. My intuition allows me to be spontaneous, playful & creative.
50. My intuition helps me appreciate the beauty & understand the truth.
51. Following my heart's desires brings me lasting happiness.
52. I have a healthy spiritual foundation.
53. I feel safe and secure in all areas of my life.
54. I am highly attuned to the messages of my inner being.
55. My self-confidence continuously grows.
56. I know that the universe is conspiring in my favor.
57. I trust that everything will become clear.
58. I accept responsibility for my past & present.
59. I surrender to the universe, knowing that whatever happens is meant to happen.
60. I am aligned with what is best for me spiritually, emotionally, & physically.
61. I am strong and healthy both inside and out.
62. My feelings of importance, value, and self-worth are growing stronger each day.
63. I feel a great deal of satisfaction in my life.
64. I am growing in wisdom and intuition.
65. I have a strong sense of my power.
66. I respect myself enough to follow through on my goals.
67. I have integrity, which means doing what is right even when no one is watching.
68. Each day, I develop more self-trust.

69. My life is an adventure filled with goals reached and dreams fulfilled.
70. All the people around me accept & love me for who I am.
71. I know that I am a person of worth.
72. I have a strong sense of accomplishment.
73. All the people around me accept & love me for who I am.
74. I have integrity, which means doing what is right even when no one is watching.
75. My dreams are becoming a reality
76. I believe in myself and my ability to make it happen
77. Inner peace pervades all that I do."
78. The Universe is working with me to achieve my goals, dreams and desires.
79. Follow your instincts and trust your inner guidance. You can't go wrong.
80. I trust in my ability to achieve my goals.

Chapter 5: Positive Affirmations for Relationship

Some people believe that a person does not have the power to change. This is wrong! We can change ourselves to be happier, healthier, and more positive. Claim your right to prosper! You are capable of anything! Love yourself and love others as you would love yourself. Talk with people warmly, appreciate them and look for their best qualities. This will benefit your relationships. Be positive, happy and energetic. Say no when you need to protect your health and your projects. Be a good friend to yourself and others. Remember that your relationships are important. Be dedicated to what you are doing and believe in yourself. I am capable of anything!

It matters where you start from and what your intentions are. Start from a positive place with positive affirmations and repeat them to yourself. Affirmations work best when your intentions are clear and firmly in mind so that you do not have to stop and think about them, unable to continue the process of self-development. Think positively! Affirm out loud three times a day (morning, noon and night) a few sentences at least that relate to the feelings you want to experience in your relationship or situation. Research shows that it takes about three weeks to develop a new habit. Don't think you have to say affirmations every day for 6 months before seeing the result. The most important thing is your state of mind and your motivation. The method works well, and you will see the results quite soon with some practice. It is talking and thinking differently that will bring positive results in your life.

The following is a collection of some positive affirmations for relationships. If any of these positive affirmations stirs you inside or makes you feel something, please let me know so I can update the list with more powerful affirmations.

Positive affirmations for relationship:

1. I am a beautiful Black woman. I love myself, and I accept myself.
2. I am a good friend, and I deserve all the best in my life.
3. I am a strong, beautiful and elegant woman, and I deserve all the happiness in my life.
4. I know how to be happy, and I want to do what I love, not work.
5. I am a good mother, and I know how to raise my son how he should be raised.
6. I am a good wife, and I know how to be a good companion to my husband.
7. I attract money, love and health. I am beautiful, strong and happy.
8. I love myself, and I want to be surrounded by positive people who share their knowledge with me and appreciate what I do.
9. Wealth is when you have more money than you need to survive. We can all be wealthy! Laugh at yourself and your situation sometimes; this will make you stronger! You have the power within yourself; find it!
10. I deserve much more in life than what I am experiencing now; therefore, I will change things to make life easier for me. I will start today!
11. I am ready for anything, and I know how to make my dreams true.
12. I am a woman of words, and I empower myself with the meaning of life. Words can be powerful!
13. I am beautiful, and I want everyone to see me that way. I feel beautiful inside and outside.
14. My partner and my friends love me. They all need my support, affection, understanding and words of encouragement.
15. My partner is happy with our relationship, and so is I!
16. My father loved me in his time; he could not do what he wanted because of his circumstances, but now that he is free, he wants to do what he loves in the way he was meant to live the rest of his life.
17. I am an independent woman confident of her innocence and deserving of trust in intimate relationships.
18. I am an attractive Black woman able to attract a man.

19. I am a seductive and intelligent friend who loves learning and teaching others.
20. My husband is the most wonderful man I have ever met, the best father in the world and an exceptional friend. He loves me unconditionally more than he can show in words; he needs time to express his feelings and understand mine.
21. I will take care of myself with healthy eating, exercise, rest and meditation; I deserve it!
22. My dreams might not come true immediately, but they will come true soon. I will work hard to achieve them!
23. We are blessed with so many resources that we should know how to make the best of them to improve our lives. There is enough for everyone!
24. I am the one who believes in what I do, and I want to make my dreams come true.
25. I am the one who decides and acts to improve my life. I have all the resources, knowledge and power to succeed.
26. I deserve a better life than what I have now. I will change for the better as soon as possible.
27. I deserve real love and peace in my energy field.
28. I have the power to change myself and my life for the better. I have the power to love without limits, without fear of being hurt or rejected.
29. I love being around people, sharing with them and laughing with them.
30. Love is the most powerful energy in the universe, it is stronger than anything else, and it always wins because it is love that makes this world go round!
31. Love never fails! It is my love that will give me happiness.
32. My soul mate is out there waiting for me. I will find them soon enough.
33. I love myself unconditionally, and I accept myself with all of my weaknesses, imperfections and mistakes.
34. I love myself unconditionally, and I accept myself with all my strengths.
35. I do not need to compare myself to others; they all have different strengths, weaknesses and skills. See them as an example only and admire your qualities the same way you admire theirs. Love yourself the way you LOVE them! Be

thankful for who you are and be surrounded by people who encourage you.

36. I deserve to be happy.
37. I deserve to find love and fulfill my destiny.
38. God is with me, especially loving me, and I am doing what God has planned for me.
39. All of my needs are met right here, and there is absolutely no reason for me not to be happy.
40. God has blessed me with the resources I need to succeed in my endeavors. I am completely healthy and wealthy!
41. I will love myself by saying simple but heart-felt positive affirmations daily.
42. I will not give up looking for my soul mate. I am worthy of finding them!
43. I am beautiful! I am healing myself to receive more energy and vitality.
44. I have the power to heal myself and to be healthy. I have the power to improve my life!
45. I have the power to heal myself and to be happy.
46. I am happy, and I deserve this happiness in all aspects of my life.
47. My partner is happy with our relationship. Therefore, we are a good team, and we make each other better people day by day.
48. I am not perfect, but I am doing my best in all aspects of my life.
49. I am not weak when I do not know something. Instead, I am curious to learn more about it and become an expert.
50. I can make good choices for myself.
51. I have the wisdom to ask for guidance and assistance whenever needed.
52. It is easy for me to let go of negativity in my life.
53. I attract positive people who help me on my way and heal me when life is difficult.
54. I have the power to heal myself and improve my life!
55. My dreams are coming true, and I am ready for anything.
56. I will do everything in my power to do what my heart desires.
57. I am prosperous, wealthy and healthy. I know how to reach my goals and the right opportunities to help me make the most of these gifts!

58. I have everything that I need right here, in front of me.
59. Every day is filled with an abundance of opportunities that make me happy.
60. I am a beautiful, intelligent and talented person. I deserve all the best in my life.
61. I am an attractive, intelligent and talented person.
62. I deserve all the best in my life.
63. I am a beautiful, intelligent and talented person with so much potential. I deserve all the best in my life!
64. My hopes are coming true! I am getting exactly what I want in all aspects of my life!
65. I have everything that I need right here in front of me.
66. Every day is filled with an abundance of opportunities that make me happy!
67. I am thankful to have a safe, secure home to return to at the end of the day.
68. I am thankful for each individual who, in some way, is a part of my life.
69. I feel fortunate to have a beautiful family, and I am proud of them.
70. My family has been with me through it all. I am grateful for them and don't take them for granted.
71. I am thankful for my parents, who love me and have taught me everything I needed to know. I know they did their best to make sure I was healthy and happy.
72. I feel grateful to have found a partner who understands me completely.
73. My kids give me the ability to practice patience, kindness, and playfulness. I am so thankful for them!
74. I consider myself lucky that my friends and family care for my well-being and want to see me happy.
75. I'm so happy to have my friends in my life – they make me feel like the luckiest person alive.
76. I might not always say it, but I sincerely appreciate the love I receive. I try to share most of it and am thankful for more love coming my way in the future.
77. I appreciate all those who helped in my life's journey.
78. I appreciate every person who makes it possible to get food on my table every day.

79. Every day, I meet people who share their knowledge and insights. I appreciate all the guidance they've been able to provide and am genuinely thankful for them.
80. I will be eternally grateful to every teacher who has helped me in my learning journey and made me into the individual I am today.

Chapter 6: Positive Affirmations for Career & Success

A positive affirmation is a statement that helps to believe in yourself, which is vital for success. Practicing these affirmations every day helps make you feel more confident and better able to take charge of your life.

To help you get started, we have compiled the following list of positive affirmations for women who are just beginning their careers:

1. I am worthy of respect at work
2. I am my best self when I make the effort
3. My beauty shines from within
4. My light penetrates through all darkness
5. I am independent, self-sufficient and resourceful
6. I am unique and special
7. I can achieve great things when I ask
8. I am full of power & prosperity
9. I know how to succeed in business
10. I have a creative vision, and I work hard for it
11. I know how to be a good mother & friend to others
12. My intuition guides me to my goals
13. My intuition is highly developed & accurate
14. Every day is a new opportunity for success
15. Every day I am growing more & more
16. My emotions are healthy, balanced and positive
17. I enter a room with confidence and joy
18. I have self-respect and dignity
19. I have good relationships with family, friends & co-workers
20. My happiness is a result of my hard work and dedicated efforts
21. I work hard to accomplish my goals every single day
22. With every passing day, I feel stronger and stronger
23. The beauty of my inner self radiates through every part of me
24. When I stand in front of others, they see the real me
25. The unconditional love within me draws me to my success & prosperity
26. Positive thoughts make life easier for me every day.

27. I am joyful, I am free to be myself, and I accept myself unconditionally
28. I am confident, motivated and excited about my success
29. I know how to find the beauty & joy in any situation
30. Success comes effortlessly to me when I choose to think positively
31. Being positive makes me feel more powerful than ever
32. When I focus on the best aspects of my life, everything makes sense.
33. Working hard is not enough. It is essential that I can see my progress and measure it by the results.
34. I have a direct line between my thoughts and actions. When we change our thoughts, our actions will automatically change too. If this happens with me, then others will catch on very quickly.
35. I am in charge of my own life, set my own goals, and decide how to achieve them.
36. I am the master of my life. I do not allow anyone to control me or hold me back.
37. There is always a way around obstacles in our lives, as long as we can find them.
38. I believe that nothing is impossible for me and that I can do anything if I want it bad enough.
39. I know how to handle the unexpected. Chaos is not a threat to me but an opportunity to discover new solutions and possibilities.
40. I trust myself even when things are at their worst. My inner strength gives me the power to cope with any situation, no matter how stressful or chaotic it may be.
41. I accept every challenge in my life as an opportunity to grow and learn more about myself.
42. I can learn as much from my mistakes as from my achievements.
43. I know that failure is only a temporary setback on my path to success.
44. I am not afraid of failure, even though it might be a part of the learning process and one step closer to success.
45. With every problem or obstacle, I am reminded that I have the power to overcome it and move forward with renewed energy and enthusiasm.

46. Even when things seem impossible, I always find the strength within me to rise again and keep going.
47. When I fail, instead of feeling bad about myself, I remember that everyone fails at some point in their lives. We all make mistakes.
48. I feel that I have the right to express my thoughts, feelings, and opinions.
49. My life is a success when I see myself not only as I want to be seen by others but also as the best possible version of myself.
50. With every trial and error, what I learn about myself helps me become a better person.
51. When others doubt me, it only makes me more determined to succeed.
52. Experience has taught me that sometimes the best way to solve problems is just by being patient enough to keep trying until success comes.
53. Every day is an opportunity to become even better. People who believe in themselves will always achieve more than those who don't believe in themselves.
54. I love myself unconditionally, no matter what I do or how much I make.
55. I am always learning and growing by accepting and respecting myself.
56. I am not afraid of change. Whenever a new situation arises in my life, I know that it will be a blessing because it is a way for me to discover more about myself.
57. Even the worst situations have something good to offer us if we approach them with the right attitude and perspective.
58. What seems like bad luck is an opportunity to rediscover my true self and move forward with renewed energy, passion and enthusiasm.
59. The challenges that I face help me grow stronger and better prepared for whatever challenges await me in the future.
60. I am always moving forward.
61. The more I learn about the life, the more I understand how much there is to learn about life.
62. I am constantly learning and growing, and my knowledge is priceless for me and those around me.

63. I accept that life often has ups and downs, but that doesn't mean I have to miss out on all the good things.
64. Every day, I strive to make my life better than before, not only for myself but also for everyone around me.
65. I'm learning new things every day through books and other people's experiences.
66. I have the power to choose how to create my life according to my definition and values. I know that I have a choice.
67. I make every single day count.
68. There is always something new to learn and to experience in this world.
69. My vision is clear, and I see myself achieving everything I want in life.
70. I am always willing to explore new things and opportunities, knowing that they are all part of the journey towards my goals.
71. Every day brings me closer to the bright future I am creating for myself.
72. I am confident that I can accomplish anything I set my mind to.
73. In life, you have to be willing to fail, learn from it, and try again.
74. I am the master of my destiny. I have the conviction that the future holds only good things for me.
75. Life is a beautiful journey where happiness is always right around the corner if we take the time to notice.
76. I know that failure is a part of life and that sometimes you need to go through certain situations to learn how to overcome them and make sure they don't happen again in the future.
77. I prefer to learn new things rather than to stay the same way. I want to be a well-rounded person that's good at many things, not only one or two.
78. I am always excited about learning new things and improving myself. I never see the world in black and white but in shades of grey.
79. I don't worry about what other people think of me because one day, they will understand why
80. I was born to be happy, and I will always keep my soul in a very positive space.

~~~~

Dreams are important but don't place too much on them. Too many goals, plans, forecasts, and limits will only lead to unhappiness. Sometimes life doesn't work out the way we want it to, so if you give up too quickly, you might be blaming yourself for not being able to do what is expected of you. Everyone has problems and setbacks, and it is not the end of the world if things don't always go your way. You can put your beliefs into action without a crystal ball!

We need to be strong in our own beliefs and stick to what we know is right. Don't spend your childhood and adolescence being told that you're stupid. Instead, learn how to believe in yourself and what you can do, no matter how big or small that may be at the moment. When you find your path, everything will happen in its own time because no one else has the same plan.

Many of the things you learn in life are not valid. The only thing that matters is what you believe and how you live your life. It's time to change the things that don't serve us anymore instead of the ones that make us unhappy. We need to become the people we want to be instead of those we think society wants us to be!

You have one life, and how it ends is up to you. Don't let other people tell you what they think will happen beyond your control. I am writing this to you to know that I thought of you and tried to help when you were older. I want to share my life with you and help prevent some of the problems that young women face so that we can have a better world!

You are already doing the work you were meant to do, and you will reach your destination. It's easy for women of color to feel like we aren't worthy of their dreams. We grew up hearing that we must adopt traditional standards for success to be accepted into society, but this is not true. It leaves us feeling a lot smaller than we are because it is just not natural for us to feel confident in ourselves and comfortable in our skin. This is not your fault; this is just how your family and the world around you taught you to be. You need to know that you can do anything because of who you are and not despite it. Don't let people tell you any; instead, be your own grand yes!

Wouldn't it be nice if we had complete control over our thoughts? We have the power to create any reality we want, so why don't we use that power to help our happiness? We are usually so consumed by our emotions and worries that our minds start thinking about all the negative things that could happen instead of what we want in life. If you focus on all the things you want instead of what you don't, your life will become more positive!

We have been taught that our race and gender determine our value and worth. But according to movies, television shows, and the media in general, we are not valued for our skin color or gender. By no means am I saying this doesn't exist, but that proves how much manipulation occurs in our society. Our worth is not determined by what we look like; it is determined by who we are!

We have been taught that all the power lies in a man's hands. This, too, is just false. While we should always listen to people's advice when helping us deal with our various issues, it should be in the form of helping us find our voice and not someone else's. We can create our success and work to create a better place for ourselves when we combine guidance from others with our strengths and abilities. We should become masters of our destiny

Chapter 7: Positive Affirmations for Positive Energy

In this chapter, we'll explore different ways to inspire positive energy so that you can be more focused on life and the people in it than ever before. Let go of your worries and be happy! Positive affirmations are a great way to remind yourself of your life's beauty. Energy is a form of vibration, so make sure you're bringing in and projecting positive vibes instead of negative ones. This will help you feel more confident about who you are and where you're going.

Positive affirmations for black women are what they sound like — positive statements directed toward a specific group of people. These statements help individuals realize their strengths and find ways to be strong in different situations. When using positive affirmations, it's essential to be specific with your words so that the message is clear and powerful. Positive affirmations allow you to change your focus on what's wrong or what's missing and move it to what is correct and present in your life already.

Positive energy is one of the most important things in life, and maintaining it can be tiring. Here are some positive affirmations that will help you maintain a positive outlook on life:

1. I am happy, and I enjoy what I'm doing!
2. I am proud of who I am
3. I love myself as much as everyone else does
4. Everything is going well for me, and I know that my path will lead me to happiness.
5. I have a lot of patience in everything that happens in life, even if others don't always appreciate it.
6. Today I deserve self-love and all the love in the world.
7. Today I am worthy, able and deserving of all that life offers me.
8. I am a powerhouse who maintains my energy for myself by surrounding myself with only positive people.
9. My opinion is important, my voice matters and what I have to say is valuable.

10. I release all things that are not in alignment with my truth and vision for myself
11. I can do anything if I believe it
12. Nothing is impossible as long as you are destined to do it
13. The body can heal faster than we give it credit for. There is more than enough for everyone
14. I am a light that shines through all darkness
15. All things are possible as long as I believe them to be.
16. I am blessed, loved, and worthy of everything life has to offer me.
17. I deserve the best in everything magnificent in my life
18. I love myself, and now I know how to get what the world has denied me.
19. I deserve success, joy and abundance in every area of my life.
20. I do not limit my worth to what others think.
21. I am not anyone else's property, and I can be with whomever I choose to be with.
22. Change is a part of life, and it's never too late for me to make positive changes in my life.
23. It's okay for me to forgive myself; I've been holding on too tightly for too long, anyway
24. My ambitions are limitless, and no mountain can stand independently, limiting me from achieving that goal
25. I am safe enough to speak up (even when silence would seem more "proper").
26. I'm a great woman, man and human being.
27. I am fearfully and wonderfully made.
28. I am a woman of substance that has value for the world to see; I am unique and beautiful.
29. I have the wisdom of a sage and the knowledge of an acolyte
30. My faith is strong enough to provide my foundation, and my roots are firmly planted in the ground of love
31. God is with me at all times; I can be with Him right now by simply closing my eyes or taking a deep breath
32. Life is not perfect, but it is perfectly good.
33. I embrace the world with an open mind and a welcoming heart.
34. I have the power to change my life.
35. My home is a haven where I come to restore myself and nurture my spirit

36. I have the power to change anything in my life that I don't like
37. Whether someone else reads, this makes no difference because these things are true for me.
38. I am grateful for my life.
39. I have abundant energy and vitality. I am an attractive person with a charming personality (whether I believe this or not)
40. I am a woman of substance that has value for the world to see; I am unique and beautiful
41. I am a woman of purpose and wisdom, a woman of compassion and courage, a woman of power and magnetism
42. I have the depth of knowledge needed to make positive changes in my life.
43. I am a woman of honor, beauty, wisdom and intelligence.
44. My body is healthy and fits me well because I eat carefully and exercise regularly.
45. My positive energy boosts the positive energy of others.
46. I have been gifted with a beautiful mind that has the potential to make positive changes in my life
47. I have limitless capabilities; my possibilities are limitless too.
48. I don't need to change anyone else but myself. My success lies in how I see myself, others and the world around me.
49. It is easy for me to trust my intuition; I am open to being led by it at all times.
50. I have the power of positive thinking; I always think positive thoughts about myself and appreciate everything good about me.
51. I am not a victim of circumstance; I create my destiny independently.
52. I am a woman of substance that has value for the world to see; I am unique and beautiful. My thoughts are clear, black & white; there are no shades of grey in what I think or do.
53. I am in control of my destiny, and I do not feel controlled by anything or anyone.
54. I respond to the world with positivity and love; I don't react negatively
55. I am a woman of presence and power with a magnetic personality that draws people in.
56. I am strong, independent and capable of making positive changes in my life.

57. I am enough.
58. My mind is a Divine instrument that will lead me to all that is good in life; I trust it implicitly
59. I have the wisdom of a sage and the knowledge of an acolyte.
60. I am a woman that knows what's important, and I act accordingly.
61. I have everything I need for my prosperity; all I need is to reach out for it.
62. I am wise enough to know myself better than anyone else; I will take good care of myself on my timetable.
63. I am a woman of values and integrity; I have a good mind that is always in the right place.
64. It is not my business what others think of me or how they compare me; I may have an opinion or two, but it's not theirs.
65. I know what I want in my life, and I don't need anyone to tell me what to do.
66. I practice self-care daily; I care for myself no matter how busy I may be
67. I am responsible for my happiness and the happiness of others around me.
68. I am a woman that is confident and knows exactly what she wants in life.
69. I let go of all negative things, and I am not afraid of what will happen.
70. I take responsibility for my life and the choices I make, and the consequences they bring about
71. I choose to be warm, generous and loving in my daily actions.
72. I am a beautiful woman; I know this because God told me so.
73. My faith is strong enough to provide my foundation, and my roots are firmly planted on the ground of love.
74. I don't need to be anybody's "savior" or "hero"; there are no strings attached to me.
75. I know that nothing is impossible for me if I want it bad enough.
76. I accept criticism but do not allow anyone to criticize me.
77. I am a woman of worth; I value myself, and therefore I value others too.
78. I am a woman of integrity and honesty; I do not get upset when people point out my faults.

79. My voice matters; I have the right to be heard.
80. I am an attractive person with a charming personality; my appeal is irresistible

~~~~

Positive energy is significantly more important than what we have believed. The world around us is so hostile that many people are now rejecting the idea of having positive energy. However, it is a good thing to be positive, as it can help you live your life and reach your goals more quickly than you would have done if you had no energy at all. There is a difference between wanting something because it would make you happy and wanting it just because it's yours. It can be challenging for black women to always reach for the things they want m an n y occasions. They will be determined to achieve their first goal and then would instead just let it go and continue to fight for it. However, by using this affirmation, you can start seeing things in a new light and realize that you deserve what you want in life. "I am happy." This affirmation will help those who are not happy with their lives to see that they can be more comfortable. They already know what they want in life, but they aren't yet focused enough on getting it — so they believe nothing is going right. "I am at peace with myself."

Chapter 8: Positive affirmations for feeling healthy

Positive affirmations for feeling healthy are among the most powerful things people can learn. Here are some affirmations for black women to help them feel healthy and loved regardless of race, sex, size, or circumstance.

1. I am perfect just as I am
2. I take care of my body in ways that will make me happy for a lifetime
3. The only person who can make me miserable is myself
4. Being black doesn't define who I am because it's not the only thing about me
5. My skin color doesn't have to be an issue because I have respect for myself
6. I am loved by my family, friends and community
7. I am a kind person who does the best I can to raise my children in ways that will make us all happy
8. I have enough to give everyone around me everything they need and more
9. My faith in God is strong regardless of what anyone else says or thinks
10. There is nothing wrong with being black or tall, fat or thin, white or yellowish. We are all made in His image, and we are perfect! We don't need to change anything about ourselves because He has written our perfect script!
11. I don't have to be the same person everyone else wants me to be!
12. I am not my father's or mother's mistakes
13. There is nothing wrong with me or my race; I am beautiful, loved by God, and love myself!
14. Remember that you don't need a man for all men who aren't what you want them to be. We are perfectly capable of getting everything we want on our own because we are gods and goddesses! We can do anything we set our minds to. So if someone isn't treating us right, let them go because it's okay.

Any man who does come my way will have to love me for me, and for him to do that, there has to be a bond first.

15. I am not my job, degree, or anything else like that. I am perfect in my skin and am here to be the best person!

16. When it comes to men and dating, I have enough self-respect not to be intimate with someone who is going nowhere and has no intention of being with me long term.

17. I have decided to take my life into my own hands, and I have decided to do it in the healthiest way possible. I am proud of myself and of who I am.

18. We are all beautiful people, no matter what anyone says, because we are God's children, and He loves us all.

19. I love myself for me and no one else. If a man comes my way, he had better love me with all I am. If he can't deal with the whole package, he doesn't deserve me!

20. My body is special, my mind is strong, and I am powerful, not because of what others think of me but because we are made in the image of God Himself. I am beautiful, and I will always do my best to care for myself!

21. Each of us is a goddess or a god, no matter what people say or think. We don't need anyone but ourselves to make us happy because that's what we are made for.

22. I control how my life turns out, and I have decided not to be controlled by anyone else. I will make the choices that work best for me and stick with them!

23. I am proud to live in the United States, where I can be proud of who I am, despite being black, no matter what race someone claims they are. I am proud of them, and I am proud of myself because I am black!

24. I love myself, my body and my life. I don't have to do anything that doesn't work for me because I'm black or white. We can do what we want, so it's okay if we don't fit into anyone else's categories.

25. If someone doesn't respect us, they aren't worth our time because plenty of people in the world are worth our time!

26. I am secure in who I am. There is nothing wrong with being black, tall, fat, skinny, or anything else. I have a right to be happy!

27. I have decided to do things the right way no matter what anyone thinks or says. I am making my life work the way I need it, and I am not stopping because someone else doesn't agree with me. I love myself and know that God loves me just as much as everyone else!

28. I am beautiful, and if someone says differently, they need to either get their eyes checked or get some new glasses because there is nothing wrong with me!

29. I am happy just as I am. My size, weight, complexion, and everything else about me are perfect just the way it is.

30. I am not a slave. I only have to be a slave to myself, and the only thing that I ask of myself is to do what works best for me!

31. Everyone around me is beautiful, especially my friends and family, because they are what matters!

32. I am perfect, just as God made me, no matter what anyone else says or thinks. My skin is darker than the person next to me, but that doesn't change that we have worth and value. Our differences make us stronger in ways that others can't understand. We are all beautiful people who deserve equal rights and privileges in society regardless of their race, color or sexual preferences! There is nothing wrong with being different. We are all equal, and we are all perfect!

33. I am proud to be black, and I am proud to be a woman. I love being a woman; it's not wrong to be black or tall, short or petite. We are all made in God's image! We don't have to change for anyone, even if we are different from the things or people that others want us to be.

34. I am not my sex or race; I'm just the person God created me to be. All of my sexual organs work perfectly, and I will continue with them if they do. As long as I remain in good health, that is important. I will make my own decisions without changing myself because I know that I am perfect in the person that God made me!

35. I am an individual, not a part of any other person or race or sex. We are all different, and we have to love ourselves for who we are no matter what anyone else says or thinks. To do otherwise would hurt us. It would weaken us. We must love ourselves and never change!

36. There is nothing wrong with me; I'm better when I'm a woman than a man. Each One One of us is special and perfect, but in different ways. I love being a woman, and I know that men love me!

37. I am proud of who I am, and I won't change for anyone else. The one person that matters most to me is me. No one will change how I feel about myself because there is nothing wrong with me regardless of what anyone says or thinks!

38. Everything that we do is right because there is only One One who knows what's best for us, and He made us just the way we are. If we listen to Him, then we're in good shape!

39. I am perfect just as I am, and I am here for a purpose and a reason. I have a reason for being here, and it's only through accepting myself as God created me that I will be happy.

40. I believe that you can do whatever you want to do if you believe it, then do it! You don't have to change what you are! Don't let anyone tell you that there is anything wrong with how you look or feel. There is nothing wrong with the way that you dress or the way that you talk. What someone says doesn't matter. You're the only One who can decide how you look and what you do. You have to be who you are, more than any other person could ever be.

41. You have to believe in your dreams because without believing them; they won't come true. Your dreams are just as important as anybody else's, so if you want something bad enough, then go out there and get it! You deserve everything that you're looking for and more. It's all right with God if we want things, but it's not all right with Him if we don't do our best to get them!

42. I love myself just like God loves me because I'm black and a woman. I'm so proud to be a woman because we can do things that men can't do. We give birth to new generations, and we are the ones who bring life into the world. I always know that I'm doing what I'm supposed to be when I give birth and raise my family.

43. I believe that God is black, and He is for us, not against us. That's why we have black skin, dark hair and brown eyes. He made us be the way we are. If He didn't want me to be this way, He never would have made me! I love my black skin, and

I will never change because I am proud of who God made me be.

44. I am proud of who I am. I'm proud of the color of my skin, the texture of my hair, and the size and appearance of my body. There is nothing wrong with being black or brown or yellow or white or red. Each of us is made for a purpose, and that purpose is to help God by loving Him, His people and everything that He created. We are part of the creation of God, and we must let ourselves be used to spreading His love in the world.

45. Our beautiful brown skin, dark eyes and black hair show God has created us. I will never change because there is nothing wrong with being black, brown, yellow, or white. I am proud to be black because it's not wrong for me to be!

46. There is nothing wrong with being different! We are all different from each other, just like there aren't two same colors in this world, but there are different colors that make up our whole world.

47. I am amazed by the world around me. Each new day provides a unique opportunity and a new gift for which I am grateful.

48. I am thankful for this feeling of gratitude – I know it leads to joy, mental peace, and the life of my dreams.

49. My sense of gratitude expands my perspective and helps me appreciate all the different ways of living, thereby leading to my happiness.

50. I live a life of gratitude and am always thankful for the help and support from those who have cheered me along the way.

51. I am grateful for the positive things in my life.

52. I am grateful for the abundance I have and the abundance that's on its way.

53. I understand how lucky I am to have so many people who care about and admire me.

54. I am grateful for my patience.

55. I am grateful to the Universe for always putting me in the right place at the right time.

56. I feel grateful for my ability to manifest my dreams.

57. I feel fortunate to have multiple sources of passive income.

58. I feel fortunate for all the luxuries that surround me.

59. I feel thankful for my unlimited financial abundance.

60. I feel thankful for the fantastic opportunities that have come my way.
61. I am thankful for the enormous success that I am constantly achieving.
62. I am thankful for my past experiences, as they have helped me evolve.
63. I feel thankful for all the positive and loving people in my life.
64. I am grateful for the love I receive every day from everybody.
65. I feel thankful for my unique friends.
66. I feel thankful for my caring spouse.
67. I feel thankful for my respectful children.
68. That helps me maintain my composure in challenging situations.
69. I am thankful for getting another chance to make my life better today.
70. I am thankful for being able to love myself and others.
71. I am grateful for my wonderful life, overflowing with so many blessings.
72. There is nothing wrong with me! There isn't anything wrong with you! We are both perfect as God made us, and we are beautiful! We must remember that we are not women or black or brown or yellow or white, but we are all. We have to be proud of who we are.
73. There is nothing wrong with how I feel about myself, I am a woman, and this is my body. I know exactly what works best for me. If it's getting up early before everyone else and going to work, then that's what I will do. No matter how others may feel about it, they can never change my mind because they don't know how my body feels.
74. The one person that matters to me is me! I love myself and who I am, and no one else will change my mind about being who I am.
75. I am black, and nothing that anyone says or thinks could ever change that.
76. God made us just the way we are because there is nothing wrong with us for being who we are.
77. We have long curly hair, brown eyes, dark skin and a dark brown complexion. There is nothing wrong with being different because we are all different. I am so proud to be a

woman because I feel that we can do things that men can't do. We seem to be stronger than they are, and they don't seem to have the same capability to love.

78. I am proud to be a woman! There is nothing wrong with my God-given body, and everything that He created for me works perfectly for me. If it didn't work right, He would've made me differently.

79. My hair is one of my best features because it's a special part of my body and identity. The color of my skin and the texture of my hair are just as important to me as the rest of me because I am a woman!

80. I am proud that I am black, and there is nothing wrong with my dark brown skin and dark brown eyes. God is black too, so there is nothing wrong with our color. It's not wrong to be black, brown or yellow or white. We are all different from each other, like there aren't two same colors in this world.

Chapter 9: Positive Affirmations for Weight Loss

Positive affirmations for weight loss can be a great tool to help someone lose weight. It's important to have positive affirmations at the top of mind when one is in a state where they are grumbling about what they would much rather do. Weight loss affirmations such as "I deserve to be healthy and vibrant" can be trackable by making them into hashtags on Instagram, Facebook, and Twitter. But it can also mean something different for a black woman who may already feel oppressed by those around them because it's another way of saying that your beauty transcends stereotypes and that you should not change your natural hair or skin tone for anyone else but yourself. It's a tool that helps you achieve your weight loss goals and helps you maintain them.

Black women have a robust and muscular body admired by many. However, not many know that the fat from dieting is more harmful than the fat that naturally comes with our genetics. The way you eat affects your body in more ways than one. If you are always on diets and hate them, this chapter will help you learn how to lose weight quickly. There are many ways to get yourself into a positive mindset, and affirmations for weight loss are one. If you are tired of losing and gaining all over, this will help keep you on track and get your mind in line for time for maintenance and other goals.

I will not share a list of affirmations for weight loss here. Instead, I will teach you how to put into action all the great advice that has been in this chapter. During my years of experience as a personal trainer, I have found that most people make several mistakes when trying to lose weight: They diet but do not know what they should eat.

You do not know what effect you're eating habits have on your body. They try to diet but do not have the willpower or the resolve to stick with it long enough. They fail because they think their body is stubborn and will always be fat no matter what they do. They do not know how to eat right and keep an eye on their diet.

You do not have enough energy to complete physical activity. You only exercise once or twice a week. Make sure you choose the right foods based on your goals and not one of the many fad diets that create false hopes for many women. Just because something worked for someone else does not mean that it will work for you. Do some research on the food and any related nutrition issues so that you can have more energy to complete a workout or other physical activity and so you will be able to lose weight quickly. Do at least three small meals per day instead of 2 big meals.

Doing a full workout every day is not recommended if you are not used to it. Do at least 30 minutes of physical activity and a lightweight training routine. You can do a quick workout and go to the gym after your day is over to do more exercise. If you have been slacking in your practice, try more intense workouts and quick ones to get yourself back on track when it comes time for maintenance. It does not matter which you choose. Just do your best to exercise at least three times a week for the rest of your life. Remember that you will not lose weight overnight, but if you are committed to this, you will achieve your goals and keep them healthy to admire your muscular body. Have patience and confidence in yourself because if anyone can do it, you!

The future is yours. All you have to do is believe in yourself and make sure that you stay positive throughout the entire process. Once that happens, losing weight will become a lot easier for you when it comes time for maintenance or other goals. This is not something that you have to do right now, so take your time. Find a way to incorporate all of the advice and tips. Slowly but surely, you will lose weight fast and keep it in a healthy range.

The period will determine the length of your journey to reach your goal weight. This is not an overnight process, but instead, a gradual one where you slowly start and work hard to lose weight in the end. This chapter teaches you how affirmations for weight loss can help you lose as much as 15 pounds within 30 days, which is suitable for starting slowly. Remember that some things we do affect our bodies more than one. If you're going to try something faster and better, look at the many fad diets.

Negative affirmations for weight loss can make you feel bitter about the process or discouraged. Taking charge of your life and your body takes time, so it is easy to give up on your journey when something gets in the way, but even negatives are positive moments that can be utilized to turn them around and keep moving toward what you want with purpose. Positive affirmations for weight loss can be hard to remember and repeat many times throughout the day. It is a PROCESS that requires some room for error and understanding of what you are working towards. If you tell yourself nothing but positive affirmations, you might lose sight of reality, but it could psych you out if you tell yourself nothing but negative affirmations. The process is not easy, so personalizing your weight loss plan to fit your situation will allow you to be more successful overall.

There are plenty of ways to go about doing this by changing up the words and altering them with specific goals in mind:

1. You are your person, and nobody else will care for you.
2. You deserve to look better than this.
3. This will be a positive experience.
4. You will achieve the body you want.
5. You can lose weight.
6. You will look better than ever.
7. I am beautiful just the way I am.
8. You will look great when you get there.
9. I can lose weight.
10. I can eat better and be more active.
11. I will gain back the weight I lose.
12. I deserve to look like this.
13. This is temporary, and it's allowed.
14. These additional fat cells will make me look fit.
15. My body is healthy now.
16. All white people are beautiful, and so are all black people.
17. My body looks good now. It's healthy, strong and fit.
18. My skin color isn't an issue. I'm a beautiful person.
19. My hair doesn't define me.
20. I'm healthy and vibrant.
21. I am sick if I'm this thing.
22. As I lose weight, my body will be healthier.
23. I already look good in this clothing. Why should I change now?

24. I am looking good, and it's temporary. It will go away.
25. I am going to look fabulous after losing weight because no one will take care of me if I don't take care of myself.
26. I'm taking charge of my life, health, and body.
27. I don't want to feel this way, but I will be healthy.
28. I deserve to be healthy, and I'm going to live to see my children grow up.
29. If I eat better and exercise, this will all disappear.
30. I know I am healthy, but I need to lose weight because otherwise, what people say about me is true.
31. I'm looking great now. It's temporary.
32. This is a great opportunity for me to take care of myself.
33. I don't want this, but it works for me, so there's nothing else I can do.
34. This is temporary, and it's allowed.
35. There are many more positive affirmations for weight loss than negative affirmations. Some negative weight loss affirmations can lead to suffering and failure, but they can also help motivate you to be positive and get the job done.
36. I will not lose weight or change. I am comfortable with myself.
37. This is good enough for me. I look great this way.
38. I will always be fat and happy.
39. I want my real size back.
40. I'm comfortable fat and happy with it.
41. I'm fed up with diets that don't work. It's a waste of time, money, effort and food.
42. My body isn't made to squeeze itself into too-small clothing. I'm fat, and I like it.
43. I've always been fat, and I don't want to be thin because this is comfortable.
44. I'm going to let myself go. I'm sick of trying to be thin.
45. I'll never learn how to take care of myself.
46. My body looks bad now. It's unhealthy, weak and unfit.
47. I'll never learn how to take care of myself. No one will take care of me if I don't take care of myself.
48. Why would I change myself? It works for me, so why should I change?
49. I've tried many times before, and nothing worked. I won't change now.

50. I'm afraid of losing my fat, and I'll do anything to avoid this.
51. I'll always be fat and happy like that. I don't want to change.
52. Why would I want to lose weight? It's ugly and embarrassing.
53. I deserve to be fat and happy.
54. I hate to diet, but I don't know what else to do.
55. I've already tried dieting, and nothing worked. I want to quit it now.
56. Why would I want to lose weight? It's ugly and embarrassing.
57. Why would I want to be thin? It's unhealthy and weak.
58. Really, why should I change myself? This is the way it is supposed to be.
59. Have you ever heard the saying: "Who you are speaks so loud that it can't be ignored? What you say is important, and it will be heard. So use your voice right now. Speak up loudly and with confidence so that others can hear your words. The strength of your belief will touch them, and they will be inspired to take action.
60. I have control over my life and my body. I am responsible for my appearance as well as my weight loss. It's up to me what I look like and how I feel. This is the way it's supposed to be.
61. Even if I don't know it yet, I have control over my life because this is difficult for me right now. But eventually, I will be in total control.
62. I am a beautiful woman regardless of what I look like. I will be a beautiful woman regardless of my appearance when I lose weight. This is what I want, this is what I deserve, and this is the way it's supposed to be.
63. I am in control of my life, even if it doesn't feel that way right now. Some things can get me out of control, but others can make me stronger. This is just one more challenge that makes me stronger. If I have to do something difficult, I need to do it.
64. I am in control of my life no matter how hard things seem right now. If I haven't been able to do something so far, it doesn't mean that I never will be able to do it. I have to keep working at it until the right time and the right moment come up.
65. I am in control of my life. That's what makes me a separate person from all others. My name is Mary, but that doesn't mean that I have control over my life and will lose weight. But

who is the real Mary? The one with the weight problem or the one with the ability to change her life and body?

66. I am in control of my life because this makes me different from all other people on earth. I can change my body and my life. If I were not in control of my life, it would mean that I was not different from other people on this earth.

67. I am in control of my life. I am a strong person, and I know that things can be hard for me for a long time, but eventually, I will overcome them.

68. Today, hard work will get me ahead. I'll be rewarded for the effort that I put in.

69. My mind knows the right things to say or do at the right time whenever they're needed.

70. My mind knows how everyone feels.

71. I am sure that what I want is coming to me.

72. I have the innate ability to become whatever I desire to become.

73. Whatever happens, it will be for my highest good

74. I am in control of my life no matter how much it hurts or how much it seems difficult for me.

75. This is what my body was supposed to look like because this is what the doctor said that I should weigh. This is this number, and everything else doesn't matter. If I want to change my body, I have to change what the doctor says I should weigh.

76. I will be happy the way I am, no matter what anyone thinks about me.

77. Everyone loves me, and when they're around, everything is a joy!

78. I feel great!

79. I am thankful for my mental strength and courage

80. I am proud of my body changes

~~~~

When trying to lose weight, people will say negative things about you. That's just how it goes. You have to be strong and confront them by saying: "That's okay. Let them say whatever they want to me. It doesn't make sense to follow their advice because it doesn't work for me. "

Criticism happens every day, and we need only look around us at all the health and fitness professionals who have been ripped apart in public forums.

Maintain Weight Loss: Achieving long-term weight control is not easy. Like many effective treatments, it requires ongoing effort and commitment. Most people will need to modify their eating behavior and activity level for a lifetime to maintain a healthy body weight. Good weight loss will be maintained in healthy body weight through following the advice above and remaining active. When weight control is broken, it is important to remember that self-esteem and other negative feelings will return. The important thing is to know how to regain control and keep going. Positive affirmations are very useful in helping people achieve their weight loss goals, but they can also be used to maintain weight loss. Many people want to continue losing weight to look their best, but it's just not realistic to think that losing a few pounds on top of where you've been will allow you to look better than you already do.

Once aspirant starts adding positive affirmations for weight loss into their daily lives, it may be easy to go overboard with them., but over time it will become easier for someone who is dedicated to making their life a better one and losing weight by using these positive affirmations to stay on track. It is important not to feel guilty about enjoying your body simultaneously as you are trying to make lasting changes with them. One should never feel bad about themselves about anything, especially when trying to live a healthier lifestyle.

Chapter 10: Positive Affirmations for Spirituality

Do you want to get into a new habit or make a positive change in your life? Do you want to create more abundance and positivity in your life? One way that is effective and simple is by creating affirmations. Your affirmation might be "I am healthy" or "I am creative." The power of positive affirmations for a black woman starts with the noise around us. What does "you are beautiful" mean if it's not being said because it's not seen? It begins with yourself, and then it's contagious. Affirmations can help empower you instead of judging you; it requires no money and takes no time.

The power of positive affirmations for black women:

Affirmations are simply a statement of truth. It is an affirmation that you believe in. Its purpose is to make the positive become your reality. It should be a statement that makes you feel good, and anything else will not be practical; if it makes you feel worse, it won't work. Like affirmations for weight loss, our negative thoughts will kick in and negate the positive statement before we even have time to act on it. So start with a positive affirmation and write it down or say it daily, like your motto or belief.

The negativity from the past and present will appear before you; this is normal; it is a part of us being human. You will have negative thoughts from the past; your family was negative, and so am I. We only have one life to live, so we better put all our energy into living it as best as possible, which means not dwelling on what has been done in the past; start afresh. This means that you need to be understanding. No matter what has been done to you or done wrong, please don't hold on to it; forgive and move on.

The affirmations include positive mantras, positive affirmations, and positive declarations. The positive affirmations key to working for black women:

The fundamental affirmation: "I am healthy," is very simple; however, it takes time, consistency, and repetition to become a habit. However, once you've made that habit, the result is fantastic. When you start to get into saying this affirmation daily, it will start coming to you automatically. Try putting on your headphones and listening to music while repeating this affirmation. Make sure it's slow and relaxing music; the endorphins from the music can help create feelings of positivity within your mind, thus allowing you to feel good every day.

Even some nature sounds can help too.

1. My life is a blessing.
2. The Universe shines its pure light on me.
3. Finding enlightenment comes naturally and effortlessly to me.
4. I am free.
5. I can tap into the source of energy at any time.
6. The Universe guides me on anything and everything divinely.
7. I am a channel for inspiration.
8. I am pure.
9. Today, I am closer to the Universe.
10. I am on the path to enlightenment.
11. I breathe in the light of God.
12. I am responsible for my spiritual growth.
13. I acknowledge God in every creation.
14. I am kind to all living things.
15. I have faith in the divine plan of the Universe.
16. I am an eternal and infinite being here on Earth to learn my lessons.
17. Spirit is always guiding me.
18. I release all the blocks to my spiritual connection and embark on my journey to self-realization.
19. I am grateful for all the incredible blessings in my life.
20. I let go of fear so that I'm ready to realign.
21. I know that the Universe has my best interests in mind, and I am receiving all I need to succeed.
22. The wisdom and knowledge of the Universe live inside me.
23. I am a divine being.
24. I am far more than my thoughts and feelings.
25. I know the Universe is guiding me toward the highest good.
26. I feel secure in the arms of God.

27. God's love is flowing through me now and always.
28. I am a divine expression of God.
29. Positive energy flows to and from me.
30. My spirit is whole.
31. I am the light in all situations.
32. I am love.
33. The power of God moves my spirit.
34. I beg for forgiveness from those I may have wronged and forgive all those who have wronged me.
35. I am His, and He is mine.
36. When I love others, I receive even more love from them in return.
37. I unlock my heart and mind to the perfect love of the Universe.
38. My spirit is at peace.
39. I view my obstacles as opportunities to get closer to God.
40. All my thoughts, actions, and words are guided by divine power.
41. I derive happiness from the Universe.
42. All is well in my life. I am immensely blessed.
43. I'm ready for the Universe to lead me.
44. I am connected to the Universe.
45. I am holy.
46. I allow the Universe to function through me.
47. My spirit is enlightened.
48. I am in sync with my inner guide.
49. I am rooted in Mother Earth's energy.
50. I always listen to my inner compass.
51. I'm willing to learn through love.
52. I emanate peace and love.
53. I share my joy and love with those who thirst for peace.
54. Everything happens at the right time, and I'm happy to live this journey.
55. I am with God, and God is with me.
56. The Divine Spirit is present and guides me at every step.
57. My life is full of gratitude and compassion for God.
58. My energy is in tune with the Universe.
59. My heart is tranquil.
60. Divine light permeates every particle of my being.
61. The Universe provides for all my needs.

62. I believe everything in my life is working for my highest good, and I'm receiving all that I'm meant to have.
63. I am a spiritual entity having a human experience.
64. I take a step back and let the Universe lead the way.
65. I unlock my mind and heart to the guidance of God.
66. This world is my classroom, and the people are my assignments.
67. My true strength lies in the present moment.
68. I feel the power of divine love.
69. I shine my light on those around me.
70. I am made of the light of the Universe.
71. My spirit and courage are unwavering.
72. I'm ready to lift the veil of the spiritual realm.
73. I believe religion to be a way of life. It is a way of living an ethical life.
74. I am aligned with my higher purpose.
75. I am a kind, loving, and spiritual person.
76. I let go of fear and pain.
77. I live in love.
78. I am an extension of the Universe.
79. I embrace the bond I share with all life forms on this Earth.
80. The healing power of the Universe flows through all the cells of my body.

Chapter 11: Positive Affirmations for Achieving Goals

Every problem is an opportunity in disguise. When everything seems to be going wrong, this is the perfect chance for me to see that what I'm made of is not bad. It's up to me to determine why it happened and use the lessons from my difficulties as steppingstones to become better. The dire events in my life are there for a reason only if I make them so. If I choose to make bad events in my life into learning opportunities, then they become that instead.

Achieving prosperity is easy when you bring the right attitude and have a positive mindset. It's easy to accomplish anything when you understand that no one is giving you anything and that everything comes from your hard work and determination. If good things are hard to come by, then it's because I haven't worked for it yet; if I keep trying, then the outcome will be what I want to be. It's hard to achieve every goal because I don't put in the necessary work and effort. I am ready to change my mindset if it means having to work harder to get what I want.

Every time something terrible happens, it's up to me to find a way to turn it into a positive outcome. If a bad event has happened, then it means that there is an even better one on its way. There is always a silver lining behind every cloud, and it is up to me to spot that silver lining so I can bring positivity into my life. If there is nothing good coming out of bad situations, they are not worth going through.

I am ready to have the life that I want to live. If a positive future is hard to come by, my thoughts and beliefs are blocking me from receiving the abundance that I truly deserve. My negative beliefs and pessimistic outlook on life are holding me back from becoming successful and wealthy because they have become my reality. If I want more success in life, it's time for me to change these beliefs and get rid of these negative thoughts so that prosperity can flow back into my life like a river flowing into an ocean.

Every time I reach a goal, it feels great. However, reaching a goal quickly goes away, and an even bigger desire or goal arises from its ashes. When I face a new challenge in life, I open the door to unlimited opportunities. There is always a more significant income level and a higher standard of living waiting for me when I set my mind. However, when I reach one of my goals, there is no time for resting on my laurels because there are always higher levels of achievement to reach. If reaching one goal is excellent, reaching another will make me feel even better.

I am the creator of my reality. I have the power to manifest my desires to become what I want to be and have what I want in life. The world is full of endless possibilities, so there is no reason why this one cannot be improved or changed to suit my needs and preferences. If what I want isn't available, it's up to me to make it so by surrounding myself with the things I need or want.

If a bad event has happened, then it means that there are better ones on their way, so it's best not to dwell on the negative one too much.

1. I am fully committed to my goals and my dreams.
2. I make it happen.
3. I am worthy of what I want in life.
4. I know that if I keep at it, then success is inevitable.
5. I deserve the best, and so does everyone else!
6. Things always work out for me when I believe in myself!
7. If this is right for me, it will happen; if not, it won't. So either way _
8. It will not occur.
9. Whatever I want to do, I am sure I can do.
10. I should have, but I don't, so let's get it!
11. I am responsible for the success of my plans, and they are working fine "my way!"
12. My life is as important as everyone else's, and no one can take that away!
13. No Matter What Happens to Me, Where I Go, Or What Life Shows Me, The Sun Will Shine, And the Rain Will Fall. The Sunshine Will Come Back Again, And the Flowers in My Garden Will Bloom!

14. It might be a tiny seed. It might be a little flower. It might be a little weed. Whatever it is, it will grow to be the flower of my life!
15. I'm ready to start living that way!
16. Even though it was rainy, cold, and gray today I fully expect tomorrow to be sunny, warm, and bright.
17. I have accomplished everything I have ever wanted in life, even though sometimes I did not believe it was possible. As long as what I am aiming for is right for me, it will happen; if not, it won't. It will work out for my best, no matter what happens to me, how I feel, or what I do.
18. You are the universe to me! Everything you have given me so far has worked out beautifully.
19. Don't give up on what's right for you because no one else knows yet.
20. I have been happy all my life. I think that is why I am so glad all the time.
21. I will always know when it is right to celebrate and when it is right to mourn.
22. It might be a tiny seed. It might be a little flower.
23. If you want something, you will get it; if you don't like something, it won't happen.
24. If I keep on trying, then I am bound to succeed someday.
25. You are the universe to me! Everything you have given me so far has worked out beautifully.
26. I have lived in every area of life; I have even lived in every body cell.
27. There is no such thing as "too much" success! As long as what I am aiming for is right for me, it will happen; if not, it won't.
28. Achieving goals, while sometimes frustrating, is a perfect thing.
29. I want what is best for my family and me, so I will do whatever it takes to achieve that goal!
30. No matter how dark it gets in this life, I can die happy knowing that everything has worked out for the best.
31. Things are happening the way they are supposed to in my life; now, even if they don't happen the way I would like, I can enjoy the ride anyway.
32. My future is bright.
33. I am dedicated to achieving my goals.

34. The best is yet to come.
35. I am taking immediate action to achieve my objectives in order to live the lifestyle I want.
36. I will reach my goals.
37. It will all be figured out.
38. I am open to all possibilities that lead to a greater purpose.
39. There is hope.
40. My dreams matter.
41. I'm going to work hard.
42. I can. I will - end of the story.
43. I am free to create my reality.
44. I won't compare my behind-the-scenes to someone else's highlight reel.
45. I am almost there.
46. It might be difficult, but I am destined for greatness because of my design.
47. My possibilities are endless.
48. I will allow myself to evolve.
49. The very fact that I exist in this world has the potential to make a difference.
50. I will trust my process and applaud myself for my progress.
51. I won't give up.
52. I won't get stuck.
53. My future perfectly represents what I see myself to be right now.
54. Every day, I wake up and know that many challenges will be faced. Yet, I'm determined to keep going and do my best to become a better person than the day before.
55. I'm grateful for all the fantastic growth opportunities that have come my way.
56. I am certain that my efforts will be rewarded, and for this, I am grateful.
57. I am lucky because my dreams and desires manifest in everything I do.
58. I am powerful.
59. I am focused on my goals, not on what's happening.
60. My thoughts inspire positive feelings in my body, and those feelings motivate positive actions.
61. I am open to new possibilities in all areas of my life.

62. It is when I let go that a higher power can guide me.
63. Everything I do reflects my light onto this world
64. Accepting others in their unique greatness can we all be better than now.
65. Power, victory, and joy come from within me.
66. I am a source of strength and radiance to all those around me because they perceive the blessings that flow from me every day.
67. We are here to cultivate our wisdom, virtues, skills, and talents.
68. I am thankful for the many blessings, both seen and unseen, in my life .
69. My dreams are becoming a reality.
70. I feel a great deal of satisfaction in my life.
71. My power and creativity are reflected in every action that I take.
72. I am thankful that I can spend my money on things that bring me happiness.
73. I am grateful for my past experiences since those experiences made me a better person and improved my life.
74. I am grateful for all the new experiences that I'll have in the future.
75. I feel grateful for everything that I have right now.
76. My goal is to live a grateful and fulfilling life.
77. I am fortunate that I can do what I love and make a lot of money doing it.
78. I'm grateful to work in a job that pays well and provides me with a sense of fulfillment by the end of the day.
79. I am thankful that I can learn new things and thus develop and grow in the process.
80. I am thankful for the goals I had yesterday because they are today's reality.

Chapter 12: Positive Affirmations for Overcoming Obstacles

Many black women have been abused, raped, disrespected, and victimized by men much more robust than them. The results of this abuse are that they feel worthless, ugly, and unlovable. They give up on themselves and feel degraded because they have been made to believe that they are no good. They have lost their self-esteem and self-confidence.

With all the challenges that black women face in our society, we need to be more aware of the social effects of our abuse and victimization to heal ourselves and grow into strong, beautiful women who will make a difference in our communities. To heal ourselves, we need to understand how our mind works and how the negative thoughts have conditioned our minds. To build self-confidence and self-esteem, we need to develop a positive mindset. It's like having a garden of thoughts or having a positive or negative way of thinking. So, if you plant seeds in your garden each day, it's only natural that you'll have lots of vegetables to harvest at the end of the year because your garden has been planted with quality seeds.

So if you put good positive thoughts into your mind by reading or listening to positive affirmations for black women every day, then good things will come about in your life, and you'll be able to live your life with more peace and fulfillment. As you go through your day, affirmations can help improve your mental fitness and overall feelings about yourself.

When you repeat the affirmations to yourself throughout the day, it releases the negative energy that has been causing doubt in your thoughts. When you believe in yourself and know that you are capable of a certain goal, you will be able to push through any obstacles that stand in your way. In this chapter, I have provided some positive affirmations that will help you begin recognizing an obstacle, mentally recognizing it and working towards removing it from your life.

Many different things can be considered obstacles to your mental fitness. A positive attitude towards yourself and life is a large part of mental fitness, but it is not the only obstacle you must work with to have a high quality of life. Different physical health conditions can adversely affect your mental state. Like physical health issues, mental health problems can be dealt with in the same manner as physical health is treated, through modern medicine and research into ways to cure the problem or recognized ways to overcome it.

 Physical health problems are very common nowadays and have many different physical treatments to help deal with the problem. In some cases, the diagnosed physical health problem cannot be treated because it is too severe or requires a medical procedure that will cause damage to the body. Other times, a mental health problem causes physical issues in the body and must be dealt with for the person to improve their mental fitness. For example, suppose a person suffers from extreme depression. In that case, they may experience many different physical symptoms throughout the day, including fatigue, loss of appetite, decreased concentration at school or work and an inability to control their emotions.

Many obstacles we face in life are mental obstacles, meaning that they occur in our minds and have no physical manifestations. These mental problems may manifest themselves in different ways, from how we think about things to how we feel about certain situations that present themselves to us.

When you encounter adversity or obstacles in your life, it can be difficult to overcome them because you are mentally exhausted. You may be physically fit and able to deal with anything that comes your way, but your mind prevents you from finding a solution to the problem.

The next time you experience some obstacle at work or home, practice using these five steps and find a way to overcome any mental obstacle causing stress or making life difficult for you.

1. Think about the nature of the adversity.

Consider the obstacles around you that you must face every day to do your job or complete some task. These obstacles are usually very common, but they can be difficult to deal with because they are mental. The more closely you can relate to the situation at hand, the more solutions you can find for overcoming it.

2. Identify any patterns occurring in your life recently that could be connected to the mental obstacle that is presenting itself to you today.

3. Talk to someone about your mental obstacle.

It isn't always easy to come right out and tell people that you are having problems dealing with something, but sometimes you need someone on your side who can help you overcome the obstacle causing stress in your life.

4. Consider what type of mental attitude would cause you to overcome the obstacle at hand if it were a problem for you right now today.

5. If a mental attitude is the cause of your problem, find a way to alter your thoughts and make them more positive.

Affirmations:

1. I can do everything through Christ who strengthens me.
2. I am courageous and determined.
3. I deserve better than I am getting. I am deserving of the love, respect, and care that is my right as a woman.
4. If God brought me this far, He would get me to achieve my dreams so long as I trust Him, keep moving forward and follow His plan.
5. I can still hit a home run when life throws me a curveball.
6. I believe in miracles.
7. I can be more than just a survivor. I can be a winner. I am strong, talented, and capable of so much more – much better than anyone else could ever do for me but only when I choose to use my gifts for the benefit of others.

8. I am not broken, inadequate or inferior to anyone else or anything else.
9. I am good enough, smart enough, and have what it takes to accomplish any goal that I set my mind to.
10. All of my needs will be met on time, not on time that I think they should be completed.
11. I am the woman God created me to be, and I love myself as much as others. When I feel alone or overwhelmed by my challenges,
12. God is always there for me – through His strength, not mine.
13. Would you violate your mind? Stop every negative thought!
14. I am a strong, disciplined woman.
15. I deserve to have the best in life, and I deserve a great life!
16. I am beautiful inside and out.
17. God always gives me exactly what I need for each day.
18. God is my supply – He meets all of my needs.
19. There are no limits on my ability to fulfill God's plan for my life.
20. Everything that happens is for my good.
21. I am a wise woman, and I am in good hands.
22. My life is in God's hands. Because He loves me, He will never let me down no matter what happens. I chose to trust and follow Him when I was young. Now I trust Him every day of my life.
23. I am a blessed woman living the best life she can live!
24. My life is filled with things to be thankful for!
25. All those struggling with depression need to know how easy things can be, and if you take God at His word, everything will get better so long as you stay strong and keep moving forward – following His plan for you.
26. I know that I can do all things through Christ who strengthens me.
27. I know that whatever is happening to me – good or bad, I am blessed and happy because I know that God loves me right now, and He will never let me down – no matter what happens.
28. I choose to keep moving forward and following God's plan for my life, not because of the challenges in my life but because He Loves Me so much!

29. Outside powers can't stop my strong spirit.
30. I trust my instincts even in the face of unpredictability.
31. I might stagger, but I never stay on the ground.
32. I might make errors, yet I won't stop.
33. I'm benevolent and empathetic toward myself when I make an error.
34. Mistakes don't equal failure.
35. Mistakes don't characterize me. I'm permitted the grace of making mistakes.
36. I'm ready to discover lessons in my misfortunes.
37. I use disappointment as a stepping stone to progress.
38. The entirety of my issues has solutions.
39. Challenges are the basis of my success.
40. I rise despite the difficulty.
41. Regardless of what occurs, I remain aligned with confidence, trust, and love.
42. The universe has me covered.
43. I can do hard things.
44. I won't ever surrender.
45. I can defeat each challenge in my life.
46. These difficulties are intended to make me more grounded.
47. I have the unyielding confidence of steel.
48. These difficulties are for me to turn out to be better.
49. I will never bend before the difficulties.
50. I have all that's needed to become successful.
51. I can get over this trouble.
52. I'm grateful that the universe is attempting to teach me with the help of this difficulty.
53. An elevated degree of challenges in life implies more accomplishment throughout my life.
54. I can oversee everything.
55. I have the capacity to conquer everything without exception.
56. Nothing will stand in the way of my achieving my life objectives.
57. I'm a couple of steps from my goals.
58. I'm free from any and all harm regardless of the circumstances.
59. Difficulties are new opportunities that will assist me with developing.

60. I can get across everything.
61. I'm open to every one of the difficulties in life.
62. I'm becoming more grounded as the days pass.
63. I'm learning new methods to conquer difficulties day by day.
64. My family upholds me in the entirety of my struggles.
65. These hardships will assist me with drawing nearer to my accomplishments.
66. These difficulties are building my determination.
67. These difficulties are intended for my improvement.
68. I have compelling emotional support.
69. I have every one of the abilities to conquer these challenges.
70. This difficulty will end very soon.
71. The best version of myself is just a few successes away from being a reality for me.
72. These misfortunes are intended to make me a superior individual.
73. I'm developing and learning.
74. I don't fight my problems. Instead, they are opportunities to learn.
75. I practice positivity that assists me with solving everyday issues.
76. These are minor issues in my day-to-day life.
77. If I want something, I will go after it and get it.
78. Life will be good for me.
79. I am the best at what I do, and my work is essential to others.
80. My Life is filled with plenty. I know what's necessary and what's not!

Chapter 13: Positive Affirmations for Happiness And Gratitude

It can be hard to find positive affirmations that speak truthfully to our experiences as black women. What does it even mean for a commitment to be positive? Are we always supposed to have positivity in abundance? We don't believe so! These affirmations are intended for when good things happen and negative things seem less significant. These affirmations help the wearer feel a little better and feel grateful amid hardship, which is a staple of the Black woman's experience. As a black girl, you're expected to follow specific rules that other races don't follow; why is that? It's hard being a black girl because we have been brainwashed with negative thoughts about ourselves by society. Society has told us that our hair is "nappy" and that we should feel shame for our natural look. Society has told us to compare ourselves to white women, who are considered the standard of beauty. Society has told us that we should have the perfect body, with no curves, and like a Barbie doll. I don't want any of this for myself, and I know many other black women feel the same way.

Black women are constantly being told what they should look like, how they should act, and how they should be treated by society. We need to stop using each other as tools to show others what we aren't supposed to be or can't do. We don't have to be like anybody else, and we don't have to be judged by the media, society, and our own families. We are strong individuals who need to change the way we think about ourselves; we CAN be anything we want, and nobody can tell us otherwise because they are just trying to hold us down.

Black women are highly underappreciated today, so I decided it was time to do something about it. I know that other black women out there feel the same way. I wanted to give them the tools they needed to change their lives. The more you focus on the good things in life and surround yourself with positivity, you will be happier. Here are some positive affirmations for black women, start thinking more positively today!

I am the only person who can hold me back from success. I am beautiful, intelligent, and valuable. I create my path in life. I deserve all the happiness in the world and much more. Happiness is not something that comes to me; it is something that I search for within myself every day of my life. My confidence does not come from other people, but rather it comes from within myself. I have my unique way of doing things in life. I know what it's like to have a hard life, and I know how to survive. Everything that happens to me is just a stepping stone for growth, and even better, things are soon to follow. My destiny is mine alone; no one can choose my path but for me. I am ready to take the following steps toward a better life for myself and those who surround me in my life.

I may not be perfect, but I am one of a kind. There is nothing in life that I can't do, no matter the circumstances. People often ask me why do I keep striving to be better? I choose to seek because my life is not complete until all of my goals have been achieved; there is always something more for me to accomplish. There has never been a time when I don't believe I could be successful at some part of my goal, so why should this change now?

I am beautiful, and it's okay to show that side of myself when others approve.

Everyone deserves happiness; our lives are not perfect, but we can still be happy with the things we do have. I don't know about you, but I want a life filled with happiness, joy, and positivity. We all deserve to be happy, and there are many ways we can make it happen.

Remember that every day is a gift from God, and we should always be thankful for it. You don't have to be religious to believe in God; even if you believe in something else, you should still try to give gratitude for what you have because there is always something that can be improved.

I was raised by loving parents who taught me the importance of gratitude in life, but my attitude towards life changed because of what I was taught when I got older. I started making excuses for myself and blaming others for my life not being perfect.

The following affirmations are meant to be said out loud whenever needed. They are to be repeated until it feels natural. For example, say the commitment "I am happy" 20 times before bed and then again when you wake up. It's best when you do this in front of a mirror so that you can see yourself while saying it. Some affirmations require children to tell their parents or guardian. Some are a little more complex. These are just a few that you can use for now.

We have more on the way!

1. I create my happiness by accepting every aspect of myself with unconditional love.

2. Being grateful leads to happiness.

3. I am thankful for all the beautiful things in my life.

4. I am willing to be happy now.

5. I am happy, healthy, and grateful.

6. I build the life I want with my positive thoughts.

7. I allow myself to feel good.

8. I am happy, and I know it.

9. I enjoy a life of comfort, health, and harmony.

10. I am emotionally stable.

11. My happiness is a gift to my friends and my family.

12. I am tolerant and live peacefully with people.

13. Today, I promise to surround myself with happy thoughts and feelings.

14. Today, I will attract only happy people around me.

15. I always choose to walk in happiness and love.

16. Every day, I attract circumstances that fill me with joy.

17. I find ways to bring happiness to other people.

18. The positive energy around me nourishes my body and helps me radiate joy to others.

19. When I focus on the positives in my life, I am naturally happy.

20. My inner joy is the origin of all the blessings in my life.

21. I commit to living a happy and productive life.

22. I choose the happiness of this moment and not the pain of the past.

23. The world deserves my authentic, happy self.

24. I am strong, powerful, and beautiful.

25. I am worth it.

26. My skin is the best color.

27. I am never alone.

28. I am a Queen.

29. I am fearless and worthy of applause.

30. My depression is temporary.

31. I am my only competition.

32. I am the God of my life; I create me.

33. I embrace each day with open arms and an open heart full of love for myself and other people.

34. I appreciate myself unconditionally

35. I deserve to be here now because the world needs me.

36. Life's simple pleasures bring me great joy.

37. My choice to be happy keeps me healthy.

38. The Universe is conspiring with all of its ability to bring me complete happiness.

39. I only attract happy and positive people into my life.

40. I naturally gravitate to people and situations that support my happiness and peace.

41. Happiness is my birthright.

42. I choose to be happy irrespective of my circumstances.

43. Happiness is one of my priorities, and each decision I make brings me to a state of complete bliss.

44. Every day, I choose happiness over any other emotion.

45. Even if I am feeling sad, I instantly choose to be positive and happy.

46. I have absolute control over my emotions, including my level of happiness.

47. Happiness is my true nature, and that is something I remind myself of daily.

48. No one dictates my level of happiness.

49. I am entirely responsible for my levels of happiness.

50. I am happy with the person I've become and accept myself for my flaws and mistakes.

51. I only allow positive and happy thoughts in my mind.

52. I am full of optimism and positive energy.

53. I only see smiles and happiness in the people around me wherever I am.

54. My positivity inspires people and lifts their spirits. And seeing them happy makes me feel great too.

55. The more I spend time with friends and family, the happier I feel.

56. The more I love, the happier I become. Therefore, I choose to love each day.

57. Optimism and happiness flow through my veins.

58. God supports me in my pursuit of happiness.

59. The more I work on myself and seek self-improvement, the happier I become.

60. Happiness does not originate from outside but from within me.

61. I pray for happiness, so I receive more of it.

62. Wherever I go, happiness follows.

63. I only live once, so any moment I spend not being happy is time wasted.

64. No matter what others say about me, I always stay happy and love myself.

65. Happiness and love are the major driving forces in my life.

66. I define what happiness means to me, not anyone else.

67. Each morning I wake up, I express gratitude to the people I love, thus making me happy.

68. I forgive others and don't hold grudges since I know such negative emotions get in the way of my happiness.

69. I only focus on things that are beneficial to my happiness.

70. I enjoy being a happy black woman and never feel guilty about it.

71. I let go of thoughts that get in the way of my happiness.

72. I reflect on my past to learn from my mistakes and not beat myself up. This habit helps me stay balanced.

73. No matter what mistakes I've made in the past, I deserve to be happy.

74. I'm not a reflection of my circumstances; I'm a reflection of how I react to them. When I choose healthy reactions and generate happiness, my life becomes better and more meaningful.

75. My purpose in life is to be happy, and I remind myself daily.

76. I keep meeting people who want me to be happy.

77. I pursue my passions since it makes me happier.

78. I engage in self-care routines that help me find peace and regenerate.

79. I cannot tolerate negative people in my life.

80. If anyone gets in the way of my happiness, they fall out of my life with ease.

Chapter 14: Positive Affirmations for Gaining Confidence

There are plenty of ways to boost your confidence. Affirmations are a great way to start. Here is a list of phrases you can say aloud or write down to feel better about yourself.

1. I am healthy, radiant, brilliant, courageous, and beautiful

2. I have a good life, with beautiful people in it.

3. I'm a treasure, and I'm thrilled to be alive.

4. Life is full of beauty.

5. I feel fortunate to be alive.

6. It's easy for me to make new friends and enjoy the company of others.

7. Every day in every way, I am getting better and better!

8. My health is excellent, and my body works perfectly; I am strong!

9. My mind is calm, clear, peaceful, and happy.

10. Life loves me; it's easy for me to love Life back!

11. I'm grateful for everything that comes into my life.

12. I'm a great person, the best I could be.

13. I love myself and those around me.

14. My Life is filled with infinite blessings.

15. Every day, I have so much to look forward to!

16. I deserve a wonderful life! Life is good to me!

17. Life will be easy for me; it will always be pleasant and exciting.

18. Life is beautiful, and my days are filled with happiness and surprises.

19. I am a success, and it's easy to make money.

20. I have a fantastic job that pays well.

21. Every day is an exciting new adventure!

22. The world is filled with possibilities and opportunities.

23. I am well-liked, so it is easy for me to get along with others.

24. Every moment of my life is beautiful and enjoyable!

25. I am enjoying the best of everything right now. My Life is marvelous and intense!

26. When things go wrong, they always turn out OK in the end! It will happen as it should.

27. I'm a winner.

28. I win every time I try!

29. I can always find the positive in any situation.

30. If it's meant to be, it will be!

31. My intuition helps me to avoid any disasters and make good choices.

32. I know that creative solutions are always close at hand if I look for them.

33. Life supports me at every turn, and everything works for my highest good!

34. No matter what happens, I will handle it with ease and grace.

35. I always make the best of any situation I'm in.

36. I am very resourceful and always find a way to make things better.

37. Today, I will have the best day of my Life!

38. I will be happy with what I have today since what we have is all we can count on!

39. It's better to do something than to worry about doing it!

40. Whatever time you give to others, you have given yourself!

41. No matter what happens, it will be an opportunity for learning and growth.

42. I am going to succeed.

43. I'm destined for a beautiful future."

44. I feel strong and capable.

45. I am confident and self-assured, and I know that in every way, I am fantastic!

46. Success will come to me quickly; it's always there when I need it.

47. Every door that opens for me is the door to a beautiful future.

48. Every turn is toward my happiness and success!

49. It's nothing short of miraculous what can happen when you believe in yourself!

50. I have a fantastic future that I have created for myself.

51. What I want is coming to me!

52. My mind and body are in great shape. They exist to serve me!

53. Every day is a good day, and today will be the best day of my life so far!

54. Work goes well for me; I'm successful, happy, and content in everything I do.

55. If I want something, it happens quickly, naturally, and effortlessly.

56. My mind always knows what to do next; everything falls into place quickly.

57. I enjoy solving problems and making my work easy.

58. I'm organized, and it's easy to get my job done.

59. Good things happen to me every day.

60. There is always hope as long as I live; all is never lost.

61. I am loved, cherished, and supported by those around me. I have a wonderful family!

62. I easily attract positive people into my Life who enrich my existence

63. The people in my life are happy and proud of my journey

64. I am more than what happened to me; I am what I choose to become!

65. Life is abundant, and there are gifts all around us.

66. Life gives me whatever I desire with ease.

67. My experiences always serve my higher good. They help me to grow and mature into a better person. They give me the strength to become what I am capable of becoming.

68. I easily forgive myself for any mistakes I may have made.

69. I'm at peace with my past and enjoy celebrating the path that led me to this point.

70. When I look at my history, I understand it better and feel more compassion for the younger version of myself.

71. My fears are nothing more than illusions; they have no power over me. They disappear as soon as I realize that they're not real.

72. I consciously make a choice to take responsibility for my thoughts and actions.

73. Forgiveness is my choice whenever I'm hurt or disappointed by those around me. It's always my decision whether or not I want to feel resentment in return.

74. It's not important how much time I spend at work. What matters is that the job gets done effectively and to the best of my ability.

75. My positive attitude helps me create a better life for myself and others.

76. I am thankful for everything in my life, and I will not dwell on what I do not have.

77. Hard work is a part of who I am; it makes me successful.

78. I attract opportunities and people who can help me along the way.

79. Hard work never goes unrewarded!

80. Turning challenges into opportunities is my specialty!

Self-Image, Mindset, And Results

Here we will discuss how affirmations positively affect our Mindset, changing our self-image and ultimately achieving better outcomes. We appreciate the importance of praising ourselves instead of criticizing, whether in real life or online. Feel free to expand on these affirmations with more meaning; they are open to interpretation.

A little sunshine helps put the fun back into everyday life. That's why I used to watch the sun come up and lie there with a smile. When you start with a positive attitude, it's amazing how many other things in your life can improve. Sometimes, I sit in the sunshine and read my affirmations aloud or say them to myself. Hearing them makes me feel good; I imagine how it will help me throughout my day. It's an affirmation that brings happiness and joy into my life right away, not something that will happen sometime when I get older or accomplish more goals or be somewhere other than where I am right now.

You're gorgeous just the way you are right now; there's nothing that needs changing. You don't need to lose weight or be more perfect. You're already perfect. I love the way you're you; it's who you are that makes you beautiful. When I see someone who is beautiful, I always think to myself, "She's beautiful just the way she is." So being yourself and loving yourself for who you are right now is most important for your self-esteem. I love the color of your eyes. It suits you perfectly; it's not too bright or too dark. They're a very nice light brown color, like honey, with a little surprise on the bottom of the cup.

I'm strong enough to carry what I'm carrying without fear or worry. I'm smart enough to know when to ask for help. I'm confident enough not to have issues with my weight or other emotions. I'm generous enough to know that having a large helping of people's problems puts you in the line of fire for all the anxieties and worries and other negative things, so it's better not to take on those hardships or worries in the first place.

I appreciate that you love me very much right now and continuously; I count on you, trust you, and respect you. It's easy because we've been together so long; we have a long history together, making it easier to be in this relationship. You're worth more than you give yourself credit for. You're worth more than you give yourself credit for; I won't even ask you to try a little harder because I know you can do it. You've got something beautiful inside of you, and it's up to us to bring it out. Could you make the most of what we have, right?

You're a very good person. Many things in your life make you the wonderful person you are and show what kind of people other people want around them and those characteristics in others that would help them succeed or make them happy. I'm smart in ways I don't even realize. I know there's more to me than what I see and what other people see. There's always something you can find out about yourself that makes you even more special. I think of myself as dainty, delicate flowers in a garden. My inner beauty doesn't need to be shown through my outer appearance because my inner beauty is beautiful in its own right. I could never change who I am, but how others perceive me might change and become better simply from being around me.

I'm comfortable with who I am and don't need to feel like I need to be someone else for everyone else to think I'm other than what I am. I want people to know how I feel – because sometimes it's hard for me to say, so I need to show them. I like the sound of your voice. Your voice is mellow and smooth; it's not too high or low. It's a nice sound that makes me feel good when I hear it. I'm comfortable in my skin. This is who I am, this is the real me, and you should appreciate me for being this way around you. Don't try to change me or tell me something about myself that I don't like or know that isn't true about myself already.

Your life is important. You're not just a statistic; you're not just another person; you're not just another face in the crowd. You have a place on planet earth, and your life is important. No matter how many times you hear things like "you're nothing," "you don't matter," or "you're worthless" all day long because of the negative things you put out there through your thoughts and words, know that it's BS! You do matter. Your life does matter. Don't ever let anyone tell you differently!

I'm no better or worse than anyone else around me except for my attitude toward myself and others. That's the only difference between people who have good self-esteem and me. It doesn't matter what people think about me unless I let it matter; I should be able to deal with whatever comes my way and not worry about what other people think about me because it has nothing to do with the real me. I'm thankful for the things I have and don't have in my life, and there are many benefits to both, so be grateful for all things that come your way. Think positive thoughts continuously to attract positive things in your life.

I'm a good parent who loves her children very much, and they know they're loved unconditionally by me no matter what they do or say. I'm just the way I am, and I don't have to prove anything. I am good enough, and I don't have to do anything or have anything to be better than anyone else. I'm special; I deserve everything good in life and as much as I possibly can take. Don't ever think that you're not good enough or don't deserve everything just because someone else doesn't believe you. You deserve to be treated like a queen!

I'm beautiful from the inside out; I love who I am and the person that I've become. No matter what happens today or tomorrow, I know that my value hasn't changed - and it never will, no matter how many times someone tries to change it. I love myself despite my imperfections. Those very imperfections are what make me unique and beautiful! And I like being unique!

I'm an understanding person and can often see all sides of a situation, whether it's a conflict in a relationship or a misunderstanding. I am not quick to judge someone who has misbehaved, nor am I quick to judge myself for any mistakes that I've made. Instead, I try to understand the situation from all involved perspectives. Sometimes we must learn the hard way and make mistakes to learn how we can improve our lives and the lives of those around us.

Self-Acceptance is a basic psychological need that contributes to positive self-esteem and self-confidence, emotional well-being, healthy relationships, motivation and personal growth, and physical health and resilience.

Your self-image has a tremendous impact on your Mindset and the results you achieve. You'll never be able to accomplish anything (career, relationships, weight loss) if there is not any confidence or belief in yourself. How you see yourself is a personal choice. You can choose to rely on external factors for your self-image, or you can choose to base it on personal qualities and abilities. The one thing you can't do is change your self-image. To do so would require you to change who you are.

Self-Image, Mindset, and Results Dear friends, I want to share some thoughts on self-image and Mindset working for me over the years. The independent thinking of a black woman is something we should all appreciate. Black women were instrumental in shaping the foundation of our society by contributing to all aspects of our culture and being an essential element in passing on knowledge to future generations of black people. Our work ethic and perseverance have enabled us to succeed despite many obstacles that have been placed against us at all levels of society. I believe that this is because we have always looked inside ourselves for strength and support rather than rely on external factors. We are always reminded of our worth when we look at the great struggles our ancestors overcame to get us where we are today. But just because we have endured slavery, Jim Crow, racism, and sexism does not mean that we can handle any struggle coming our way if we are not prepared. Many black women feel like their inner strength has weakened, and they can no longer stand up for themselves against even the most minor of offenses. I'm here to tell you you might be wrong. You may have been conditioned to believe that you no longer have the strength to overcome hardship, but don't give up. The truth is that external factors have weakened your self-image, and you can regain your strength.

What you do every day is a choice; your actions or inactions will reflect the person you believe yourself to be. You are only limited by the self-image of who you choose to be. The old saying still holds, "You are what you think". The way many black women feel about themselves has been affected by outside forces. A woman's self-image is a combination of her upbringing and her life experiences. This is why having the right outlook on life plays a large role in self-image and Mindset. The concept of Mindset is something that many of us don't think about often. But this concept is so important to understand if you want to be able to maintain a positive self-image and achieve your goals.

The way we think about things directly influences what happens to us. How we feel about ourselves and our surroundings will determine how much progress we can make in any given situation, regardless of the obstacles that stand in our way. Your thoughts will determine how you will often respond when tempted by certain situations or thoughts during the day or night. You may feel like you have no control over the thoughts that run through your head, but this is not the case. You have an opportunity to choose every decision you make. When you fail to act, there is a weakness in your Mindset.

There are 3 main aspects of Mindset that I want to share with you:

Attitude: Everything that happens to us in life happens for a reason, even if it doesn't seem right. When we try to understand why something happened in our lives, we can accept it better and put it in perspective. Questioning the unknown is a good thing and often leads to solutions we wouldn't have found otherwise. Most of the time, we don't understand why we are experiencing something but instead use this time to better ourselves so that our next experience will be different.

Positive Attitude: The world is full of negativity and people who try to bring you down. But with all this negativity, you can rise above the negative and be a beacon of hope for others. Your attitude determines your level of positivity. It's okay to fall sometimes; it's even okay to feel bad about yourself now and again. But, being a victim of these feelings only leads to defeat. We have all been victims of our experiences at one point or another. It's important to move forward and find a way to overcome your experiences so that they will not be as traumatic the next time you experience something.

Will: Will is the ability to decide what is right or wrong for you based on your thoughts and feelings. Will is your inner strength to overcome anything that comes at you in life. We lose will when we feel bad about ourselves because of outside circumstances. But when we have a strong will, we rise above any adversity that comes our way. We didn't come this far in life to fall short now.

If you are struggling with a low self-image, I encourage you to write out your thoughts and feelings about yourself. You will find that your perspective on yourself will change as you learn more about who you are. I will leave you with a quote from one of my favorite authors, Stephen King, that I think is perfectly suited to this topic: "There's nothing you can't do. You can be anything you want". Your choices will directly affect what happens to you as you go through life. The choices you make every day will determine the person you become and the life you live. A strong mindset is built by being able to handle yourself in any situation. Try to identify areas where your self-image could improve and surround yourself with people that are positive influences in your life. You do not have a reason to be anything but strong and positive, especially when loving yourself!

Conclusion

Use affirmation in your daily life. If you do, you'll find that your outlook on life becomes more positive, and you can think about what you want to achieve instead of what's been holding you back. It's difficult to accept that change may not come overnight, but you can make your life better with a little bit of help. There's no rush to do it all at once; think positively every day, and you'll start to see the benefits. Positive Affirmations are an essential weapon in any woman's self-care armory. They can help us through our most challenging times, big or small. They encourage and inspire us to move forward. These affirmations are specifically tailored for black women because of the unique challenges as we try to walk this life with grace, beauty, and power.